# A BRIEF HISTORY

# OF THYME

# A BRIEF HISTORY of THYME

## and other

## herbs

## Miranda Seymour

Illustrations by
Jane Macfarlane

GROVE PRESS
*New York*

First published in Great Britain in 2002 by
John Murray (Publishers) Ltd., London, England

*Printed in the United States of America*

FIRST AMERICAN EDITION

Library of Congress Cataloging-in-Publication Data

Seymour, Miranda.
    A brief history of thyme and other herbs / Miranda Seymour.
        p. cm.
    Originally published: London : John Murray, 2002.
    Includes bibliographical references (p.  ).
    ISBN 0-8021-4008-4
    1. Herbs. 2. Herbs—History. 3. Herbs—Folklore.
    I. Title.

SB351.H5S464 2003
635'.7—dc21                                              2002044684

Grove Press
841 Broadway
New York, NY  10003

03 04 05 06 07   10 9 8 7 6 5 4 3 2 1

*To our sons*
*Merlin and Thomas*

# CONTENTS

| | |
|---|---|
| Angelica | 1 |
| Basil | 4 |
| Bay | 6 |
| Burdock | 9 |
| Butterbur | 12 |
| Camomile | 15 |
| Celandine | 18 |
| Chervil | 21 |
| Chickweed | 24 |
| Chives | 27 |
| Colt's-foot | 30 |
| Comfrey | 34 |
| Coriander | 37 |
| Dandelion | 39 |
| Dill | 41 |
| Elecampane | 44 |
| Eyebright | 47 |
| Fennel | 50 |
| Foxglove | 53 |
| Garlic | 56 |
| Horsetail | 59 |
| Hyssop | 62 |
| Indian Hemp | 65 |
| Lavender | 68 |
| Lemon Balm | 71 |
| Lovage | 74 |
| Marigold | 76 |
| Marjoram and Oregano | 79 |
| Meadowsweet | 82 |
| Milk Thistle | 85 |
| Mint | 88 |
| Mullein | 91 |

# CONTENTS
## (*continued*)

| | |
|---|---|
| Parsley | 93 |
| Rosemary | 96 |
| Rue | 99 |
| Sage | 102 |
| Soapwort | 105 |
| Solomon's Seal | 107 |
| St John's Wort | 110 |
| Tansy | 112 |
| Thyme | 115 |
| Valerian | 118 |
| Woad | 121 |
| Wormwood | 124 |
| Yarrow | 127 |

# PREFACE

I was flattered but alarmed when the gardening editor of the *Independent* suggested that I might like to contribute a weekly column on herbs. The paper's Saturday gardening pages are elegantly dominated by Anna Pavord and Ursula Buchan, both of whom write beautifully and knowledgeably on every aspect of horticulture. If something I plant flourishes, it's a miracle.

Reading about herbs, rather than cultivating them, was what was proposed, the editor explained, cutting short my objections. I could do what I liked with my column, so long as I wrote about the herb in question. Odd facts, strange remedies, historical notes, rhymes, anecdotes – whatever took my fancy.

I paused. Acquiring mildly eccentric snippets of information is as enticing to a writer as catnip to a tabby: ignorance really is bliss when you thrive on curiosity and aren't ashamed to admit it. So I said 'Yes'.

The next step was to find an illustrator, a skilled artist who could fit the schedule and wouldn't mock my inability to distinguish between the foliage of, say, woad and wormwood.

Jane Macfarlane is my first cousin: at five we were best friends, sharing our baths with a wind-up gyrating frog. Our shared grandfather was an amateur rhymer (by sheer coincidence, John Murray published his five slim volumes of humorous verse). Noting our similar ages and mutual affection, he thoughtfully composed an appropriate tribute. His next collection was dedicated 'To Miranda and Jane' and the poem confidently predicted a celebrity in which his small grand-daughters would jointly rejoice. All we had to do, it seemed, was wait.

Move forward half a century.

Having Jane to work with has been a benefit which needs acknowledgement. There is hardly an entry here to which she has not contributed an idea, a story, or an apt quotation: if my description of the visual properties of a herb appears dilatory, it is because I have already seen the care of her representation.

I don't think I will ever make a gardener, but I have learned much. The herbs about which I have written absorbed me as thoroughly as characters in a book. My favourites are comfrey, tansy and woad, but how can I leave out angelica and mullein? Their histories are remarkable and I remain astonished by the skill, intuition and patience with which early civilizations coaxed the most evil-looking clumps of leaves to yield their mysteries. How did they discover comfrey's singular ability to heal cuts, or woad's to produce its rich blue dye? How did they work out that sage is a powerful mental stimulant, that wild marjoram is good for depression? Is it not extraordinary that modern research so often points us back to the similar use of a herb in ancient times?

Our joint thanks are due to Carolyn Hart, the originator of the idea for this book as a weekly column, to our editors, Grant McIntyre and Liz Robinson, to Elizabeth Stratton at the John Innes Institute in Norwich, and to Professor Dominic Scott, through whom we were made aware of the wealth of herbals held at the older colleges of Oxford and Cambridge. The universities, in their first, monastic incarnation, were centres of medical research and the colleges became the repositories of the most important works, often richly illustrated, on herbs and plants.

Our thanks are also due to the many readers who sent in comments and some valuable corrections. We hope that the end result is not too remote from the book you kindly urged us to create from the Saturday column.

## BIBLIOGRAPHY

This is an abbreviated list of the books on which I gratefully drew. Two, Dr Buchan's *Domestic Medicine* (1791) and Dr Robert Thornton's *Herbal* (1810), have never been reprinted. Aristotle's *History of Animals* is available in ten volumes (Loeb, 1991). The editions of John Gerard's *Historie of Plantes* (1597; revised 1633) and Nicholas Culpeper's *Herbal* (1653) which are most easily available are heavily abridged from the gigantic originals: to see these, go to the Bodleian or the British Library.

Deni Bown, *The Royal Horticultural Society's Encyclopedia of Herbs and their Uses* (Dorling Kindersley, 1995)

Maggie Culver-Campbell, *The Origin of Plants* (Headline, 2001)

Steven Fulder, *The Garlic Book* (Avery, 1997)

Mrs Maud Grieve, *A Modern Herbal*, 2 vols (Dover reprint, 1982)

Barbara Griggs: *New Green Pharmacy: the History of Western Herbal Medicine* (Vermilion, 1997)

Henry Hobhouse, *Seeds of Change* (Papermac, 1985)

David Hoffmann, *Holistic Herbal* (Element, 1996)

Mrs C. Leyel, *Herbal Delights* (Faber reprint, 1989)

Claire Loewenfeld and Philippa Back, *The Complete Book of Herbs and Spices* (David and Charles, 1974)

Richard Mabey, *Flora Britannica* (Chatto & Windus, 1997)

Anne Pratt, *The Flowering Plants, Grasses, Sedges and Ferns of Great Britain*, 6 vols (Frederick Warne, 1855)

Eleanour Sinclair Rohde, *The Old English Herbals* (Dover reprint, 1971)

                    Happy, in my judgment
The wandering herbalist, who, clear alike
From vain, and that worse evil, vexing thoughts,
Casts on these uncouth forms a slight regard
Of transitory interest, and peeps round
For some rare flow'ret of the hills, or plant
Of craggy fountain; what he hopes for, wins.
Or learns, at least, that 'tis not to be won:
Then, keen and eager as a fine-nosed hound,
By soul-engrossing instinct driven along
Through wood or open field, the harmless man
Departs intent upon his onward quest!
No flow'ret blooms
Throughout the lofty range of these rough hills,
Or in the woods, that could from him conceal
Its birth-place!

                              WILLIAM WORDSWORTH

# ANGELICA
## *Angelica archangelica*

THE MUSICAL NAME of *Angelica archangelica* is
linked to a legend that the herbally well-
informed Archangel Michael revealed the plant to a
monk as a certain cure for the plague. Another
story connects its blooming to St Michael's official
day, 8 May in the old Julian calendar. Yet another
convincingly suggests it commemorates the north-
erly Russian port where it was found.

Native to the northern countries of the Baltic,
angelica reached England in the mid sixteenth
century and was swiftly adopted and praised for its
curative powers. The English, however, chose not
to follow the Latvians' practice of trilling angelica's
praises while taking it to market. Of these ditties,
still sung in her day, the herbalist Mrs Grieve noted
that the words were so ancient that the Latvians
themselves had no idea what they meant.

Angelica is held in high esteem among the white-
witch branches of herbalism. A website named
WindWolf's Den tells visitors that, as a herb of
Atlantis, it will put practitioners in touch with their
'Atlantean energies, visions and understanding'.
Used in the bath, WindWolf continues, angelica
will bring 'a radiance of joyful, positive energy to
the psychic self'; carried as an amulet, it protects

from danger and brings good luck. What more could one ask for?

John Parkinson, the apothecary whose *Paradisi in sole Paradisus terrestris* (1629) won him the title of King's Botanist from Charles I, was similarly enthusiastic: angelica, he wrote, was the most valuable of all medicinal plants. Gerard, impressed by the story of the Archangel Michael's revelation, told his readers that chewing angelica root 'doth most certainly drive away pestilent aire'. He also knew of its power to protect the wearer from misfortune, and expressed confidence in its ability to cure the bite of a mad dog or a snake.

Excellent as a digestive and as a general tonic, angelica also has an intriguing reputation for promoting an aversion to alcohol, but I have been unable to discover in what form the plant should be taken to produce this effect (Alcoholics Anonymous might consider some research). Crushed, the root and hollow stem produce a yellow juice which has been used as a textile dye, but most people prefer to grow angelica for its appearance: tall and expansive, it is immensely handsome with a distinctive scent, quite unlike the sharper tang of fennel, lovage or chervil. It relishes damp and shade and its seeds float, so angelica often appears on the banks of rivers and disused canals. Walking along the Regent's Canal and out to east London one summer afternoon, I was astonished by the amounts growing on the embankment.

Mrs Grieve records it as rampaging all over Lincoln's Inn Fields in the 1930s, eagerly collected by the 'foreign population' who lived in what were then terrible slums around Seven Dials, near St Martin's Lane. The poor foragers might have been gathering it for use as a household tonic, or to be turned into candied preserve, a delicacy originating in Denmark which has been an expensive favourite in England for at least three hundred years. But angelica has other uses. Pieces of its stem, cooked with rhubarb, alter the taste into something much more subtle and interesting; an oil distilled from the seeds is sometimes added during the process of making muscatel wines; and the seeds themselves used to be combined with juniper berries in gin distillation. Vermouth and chartreuse both owe something of their curiously addictive taste to angelica.

Ready for more suggestions? Well, you can cook the young leaves like spinach, as the Lapps and Norwegians do; you can spice bread with the seeds; you can follow the Finns and bake the stems in a wood fire. You can even, so I have heard, lay them (the stems, not the Finns) in shady corners of the garden to catch inquisitive earwigs. The leaves, picked before flowering, add warm under-notes to a pot-pourri. For a digestive, pour a pint of boiling water over an ounce of bruised angelica root and drink a wineglassful three times a day after meals. This is what's called an acquired taste.

# BASIL
## *Ocimum basilicum*

KRISHNA, SO THE story goes, fell in love with a nymph, Tulasi, and turned her into a basil plant: forever after, only Tulasi's delicate sprigs were used to clean Hindu temples. In Greece, although sufficiently respected to be called the king's plant (*basileus* means king), basil was not expected to flourish unless heaped with insults at the time of sowing.

The Greeks linked basil to treachery and misfortune, a superstition which is also apparent in the Roman habit of stamping on it. Later, the Italians associated it with love and called it 'Kiss me, Nicholas'. Boccaccio put the two interpretations together after noticing the crinkle-haired look of a small-leaved basil bush (*Ocimum basilicum* 'Minimum', or perhaps 'Crispum'); his tale of Isabella and the basil bush which gives away the secret of where her dead lover's head has been buried was later famously reworked by Keats. Lovely poem: gruesome subject.

Several of the old herbals suggest basil for dieting: whoever sits before a plate with a sprig beneath it won't be able to eat a mouthful. But this scarcely fits with the fact that medieval Londoners' favourite sausages were those from Fetter Lane, generously flavoured with the herb. Basil was admired for its aromatic scent, but Moldavian girls were surely too optimistic in believing that any young man presented with a leaf would instantly fall in love with them. Tudor housewives handed out whole pots of basil to their visitors without, so far as I know, inspiring anything more than gratitude.

Basil is useful in the kitchen not only in cooking but as a discourager of flies and a modest form of ioniser. Be careful, however, to keep the leaves watered, as well as the soil, if your kitchen is warm. For a headache, rub a little oil of basil on your forehead, as you might rub oil of thyme. An infusion of basil leaves taken at bedtime helps to relieve stomach pains, especially those connected with delayed menstruation.

In Corfu, I never had to do anything to help basil grow. Planted in a pot on the terrace in early spring, it always flourished into a plump bush. There's not much chance of that happening in Britain, but one useful tip is simply to keep pinching out the new leaves as they form on the stems. With a little persistence, not much water, and all the light you can offer, the result should be a plant as tall as a shortish Indian nymph. Oh, and Culpeper says not to plant basil anywhere near rue.

My favourite basil recipe is a sauce to eat with *rigatoni* or *conchiglie*. Fry together two chopped cloves of garlic, a tin or two of chopped tomatoes and a handful of chopped basil leaves (use the larger ones: the smaller are better sprinkled in salads). Drain the cooked pasta, add balsamic vinegar to taste (about four tablespoons for two people), stir in a second handful of chopped basil, add the tomato mixture and stir again. Sprinkle with grated *pecorino*: it's gorgeous.

# BAY
## *Laurus nobilis*

BAY LEAVES – AND there's no ancient law against using them dried, from a jar – can bring you a vision on Valentine's Day. Wear a just-washed or new nightdress or nightshirt and lay the leaves on your pillow. Dab a bit of water on them, and before going to bed, recite this simple rhyme:

> Good Valentine, be kind to me,
>
> In dreams let me my true love see.

Given that the last thing in your mind before sleep often does make its way into a dream, there's no reason it shouldn't work, so long as you've someone in mind worth dreaming about.

Keats, before he knew how vicious his critics would be in their attacks, looked 'To see the laurel wreath on high suspended That is to crown our name when life is ended' (*Sleep and Poetry*), while in *Theokritos*, a best-forgotten meditation on Britain's fading imperial splendour, a patriotic Oscar Wilde lamented that 'Our little island is forsaken quite: Some enemy hath stolen its crown of bay.' The Psalms offer a more memorable image, of a wicked tyrant 'spreading himself like a green bay tree'.

Rather an overdose of quotation? Not really, since the bay's best-known connection is with

Apollo, the god of poetry. Daphne, a nymph he pursued, asked the powers of Olympus to rescue her, and they obliged by transforming her into a sweet bay or laurel (the Greek name is *daphne*). Apollo, consoling himself with a wreath made from her branches, decreed that all victors and all poets who created beauty should be crowned with Daphne's leaves. *Bacca*, Italian for berry, combined with *lauro* for laurel, gives us the baccalaureate: etymologists will not need telling that the word 'bay' itself is closely connected to the French *baies*, also meaning berries.

Bay has a venerable reputation for its protective as well as its vision-inducing properties. The Sybil of Delphi, sitting under a bay-thatched roof, chewed the leaves to induce a state of receptive trance; superstitious Roman citizens were advised to take refuge among the bay trees in the San Lorenzo area when plague afflicted the city. The death of a bay tree was always a bad sign. The herbalists Bartolomaeus Anglicus and John Parkinson both claimed that the Emperor Augustus twined bryony and bays around his bald head, 'thereby to be secured from lightning'. Lupton's *Book of Notable Things* (1575) recommended standing under a bay tree as a protection against the devil and the 'falling sickness'. Nicholas Culpeper, a sincere believer in the influence of stars upon herbs, noticed that the bay was in the celestial sign of Leo and thus unusually resistant to witchcraft. Respectfully quoting Mizaldus as his authority, Culpeper went on to declare 'that neither witch nor devil, thunder nor lightning, will hurt a man in the place where a Bay-tree is.'

Earlier, in the sixteenth century, the herbalist William Turner had a more frivolous contribution to make. Bay leaves, 'when they are casten into the fyre ... crake wonderfully', he wrote, adding almost as an afterthought a tribute to their delicious fragrance. Bay, in Turner's day, was better known as an essential component of the celebrated Venice treacle, *Theriaca Andromachi*, first made by Nero's physician Andromachus as an antidote to poison. For the Emperor's subjects, to see it being made up must have been as good as a visit to the Coliseum, since it contained more than a hundred ingredients, including such exotics as Balm of Gilead, and had to be mixed in a public place, observed by every doctor in the city. The poor man's version, known simply as 'Treacle', had only four ingredients. It is not reported whether the two were equally effective.

Bay survives shade but dislikes frost and can grow to eight feet tall in a pot, twenty-five feet in the wild. I've heard of, but never seen, sixty-foot bay trees. Drying the leaves is best done in a dark airing cupboard, over about a week, but once brown, the leaves lose their aromatic potency. In the United States bay leaves are often crushed and put in kitchen cupboards to keep out cockroaches. Bay leaves are nice in a bath, and a bay-scented candle is an effective stress-reducer. A basic ingredient of bouquets garnis, a bay leaf is also traditional in rice pudding and many other creamy or milky recipes, sweet and savoury. The following mixture, ground together and kept in a dark glass jar, makes a pleasantly spicy general seasoning:

1 tbsp celery seed; 1 tsp mustard seed; 1 tbsp black peppercorns; $\frac{1}{2}$ a cardamom seed; 1 tsp sweet paprika; 6 bay leaves; 4 whole cloves; $\frac{1}{4}$ tsp mace (ground fresh from the nutmeg's husk)

# BURDOCK

*Arctium lappa*

Burdock's finest literary hour came when Hans Christian Anderson turned its broad leaves into a forest for a haughty family of white snails whose boast was that they alone had been singled out for consumption – and in a silver dish, too – at the local castle. The leaf under which they dwelt was what gave them their singular flavour. Sushi eaters will know what Anderson was talking about if they have tasted *hotategi*, scallop wrapped in burdock leaf. Japan is now the biggest cultivator of the plant, known there as *gobo*.

Nathaniel Hawthorne disparaged burdock, sending it to keep company with pigweed and apple-peru on the neglected grass plot outside Boston's first prison in *The Scarlet Letter* and letting it grow wild beside hogweed in the neglected yard of *The House of Seven Gables*. Robert Louis Stevenson, a writer who never erred in his botanical observation, introduced it in *Kidnapped* as cover for David and Alan Breck when they were hiding out near Stirling Castle. Chaucer put a burdock leaf under the Canon Yeoman's hood to keep the sweat off his face as he rode towards Canterbury.

Bruised and applied to the soles of the feet, the leaves were still being used as a country cure for epilepsy and hysteria in the 1940s, according to Mary Thorne Quelch, a herbalist who also fondly recalled the years when a fine crop of burdock grew behind a Fleet Street hoarding. Like several other writers, she recommends boiling the young stalks, which should be picked before the purple flower has blossomed and apparently taste like asparagus – as do a suspiciously large number of herb and plant stems.

Culpeper, often so heartwarmingly sensible, is rather wide of the mark with his advice to pregnant women that they could control the position of the foetus, and the womb itself, merely by holding a burdock stalk in the appropriate position. More reasonably, he commended a poultice of the leaves mashed with eggwhite for burns, and the expressed juice from the leaves, sweetened with honey, as a diuretic. The Romans hung bags of burdock seeds around their necks to ward off rheumatism, but the plant's best medicinal reputation is as a superb purifier of the blood. Gout, caused by a buildup of uric acid, can be alleviated by a thrice-daily dose of burdock root, celery seed and yarrow, boiled together in equal proportions for fifteen minutes and then strained. Skin irritations can be calmed by a dab of the expressed sap of burdock root, mixed with Vaseline (this makes an excellent alternative to teatree oil). One old-fashioned herbal recommends the juice of a burdock leaf pounded with wine, strained and taken in a small glass morning, noon and night as a cure for eczema.

Burdock root is highly valued in China as an aphrodisiac and rejuvenator, as beneficial to the circulation as in building up resistance to tumours. A thick soup of the roots is sometimes served in Japan. Long, thin and white, they are also dug up in winter and served sliced and stir-fried with garlic and green vegetables. Little regarded now in the

West, perhaps in part because the deep-reaching roots are difficult to harvest, burdock's popularity with the Japanese is causing it to be investigated in New Zealand as an economic niche crop, both for tourist consumption and for sale abroad.

Burdock also has an intriguing history in the fight against cancer. The twelfth-century abbess Saint Hildegard of Bingen, whose chief medical work, *Hildegardis causae et curae*, was based on her own researches, is said to have used it for this purpose, and between 1930 and 1950 it was a key ingredient of the Hoxley cancer formula, marketed by a former coalminer.

Known in earlier times as beggar's buttons (for its burrs) and philanthropia (for the way they attach themselves to people's clothes), burdock is also, but more obscurely, called the happy Major. The modern nickname velcro plant commemorates the ingenious invention of a walker who took note of the way the seedheads cling to an equally rough surface. But burdock's strangest appearance must surely be in the catsuit worn once a year by the Burry Man for his walkabout in Queensferry, Edinburgh. The burrs are laid out on long tables before being stuck to white flannel garments worn by the long-suffering Burry Man as he stumbles from house to house, refreshed along the way by tots of whisky. The custom began as a way of bringing luck to local fishermen: as burrs stick to the man, so will fish stick to the nets.

# BUTTERBUR
## *Petasites hybridus*

MANY READERS WILL remember that Barliman
Butterbur kept the inn of The Prancing Pony
at which Frodo Baggins first met Aragorn, in
Tolkien's *Lord of the Rings*. Fewer may know that
the plant's large heart-shaped leaves were formerly
used to wrap butter, keeping it moist while prevent-
ing leakage. Other less attractive names include
blatterdock, capdockin and, bafflingly, bogshorns.
'Lagwort' refers to the way the butterbur leaves
delay their appearance until the pink cones of
flowers have dropped or withered. 'Umbrella plant'
acknowledges its usefulness in providing shade,
once much appreciated by free-ranging poultry on
river banks.

One old herbal claims that a butterbur leaf can
grow big enough to be used as a tablecloth: a search
through the illustrations of old children's books
would probably show just such a leaf in service for
a fairies' feast. Representations of Mercury often
show him wearing a fetching pointed cap which,
on closer examination, reveals itself as a butterbur
leaf, while *Petasites*, the name of the genus, derives
from *petasos*, the Greek word for a broad-brimmed
hat. Shepherds, in early days, used the leaves as
sunhats, and John Gerard, writing in Elizabethan

times, still knew this as a familiar sight on country strolls.

Butterbur has never been regarded as a delicacy in the West, but the buds are a tasty treat in Japan, where they are known as – careful with your pronunciation – *fuki*. Minced, reshaped and dipped in *miso*, the buds are roasted over a charcoal fire and sold at wayside stalls.

Butterbur grows both on mountainsides and around the edges of fields in parts of Japan. In Britain, the plant is usually found creeping across marshy sites, spreading its stems out from strong, fleshy roots. Butterbur has often had a bad press because of the way it creates an airless shadow beneath which nothing else will flourish, so that you could be forgiven for thinking that this is why it was known as *Pestilenzwurz* in Germany; you would, however, be wrong. The flowers of butterbur were thought to be 'a soveraigne medicine against the plague' and were praised as such in Henry Lyte's *Herbal* of 1578. John Gerard, another Elizabethan, also knew butterbur as a plague remedy, and recommended taking the powdered root. It 'provoketh sweat and driveth from the heart all venim and evill heate,' he wrote; also, 'it killeth worms', and was valued as a digestive and cough remedy.

Nicholas Culpeper tells us that butterbur seeds, when infused in wine, can lift downcast spirits. Butterbur can also be used to call them up: sow the seeds in a lonely spot on a Friday morning before sunrise; while sowing them, recite this rhyme, and your phantom true love will appear and start cutting the grass:

> I sow, I sow!
> Then my own dear,
> Come here, come here,
> And now and now!

Today, butterbur roots are back in the news, not because of their connection with *Lord of the Rings* but because it appears that an extract from them is a fairly successful cure for migraine, and recent tests undertaken in Switzerland suggest that the same extract can alleviate hay fever without the risk of side-effects. David Hoffman, in his excellent *Holistic Herbal*, also recommends a diluted potion of the powdered root as a muscle relaxant, and laying the healing grey leaves on open cuts.

# CAMOMILE
## *Anthemis nobilis*

'IT HAS FLOURES wonderfully shynynge yellow and resemblynge the appell of an eye', William Turner wrote in his herbal, but it is the sharp scent which gave camomile its old name of 'earth apple'. Not everybody likes it. 'Strong' but 'not ungrateful' was the verdict of Dr Robert Thornton, author of a herbal published in 1810; the taste, he added, was 'very bitter and nauseous'. Because it cured all rheumatic pains the ancient Egyptians dedicated camomile to the sun – 'and they were like enough to do it, for they were the arrantest apes in religion I ever heard of', was Nicholas Culpeper's tart comment. He was nevertheless ready to concede that the plant had remarkable medicinal properties.

Camomile has a dual reputation, as a cure for both people and plants. Known from early times as the plant's physician, it was esteemed for an almost magical ability, when grown nearby, to revive any plant which was wilting. Not only this: if you believe in magic, camomile in your garden will counter any spells cast against you. Since it has the magic attribute of success, punters should dip their hands in camomile-infused water before placing a bet. You'll have no difficulty in growing it, particularly if you plant it where it is most likely to be walked on:

'Like a camomile bed, The more it is trodden, The more it will spread', one old poem tells us. Victorian garden books describe how the owners of cottage gardens would walk daily over their camomile lawns to make them flourish. Sometimes it was planted on a bank or seat, for medicinal use, since sitting on it was thought to ease rheumatic pains while giving warmth to the body. Anne Pratt, a nineteenth-century plant specialist, wrote poignantly of seeing a consumptive patient 'sitting by the chamomile bed to inhale an aroma which he hopes will bring strength to the weakened lungs.'

The fields around London were bright with camomile in Tudor times, and well into the nineteenth century it thrived wherever commons were used for grazing. Now, miraculously, it is making a comeback on village cricket pitches, where the mowing and rolling is exactly what it most appreciates. Visually pleasing though the effect is, however, it is not ideal, especially for players with what has become a common allergy to plants of the daisy family, of which camomile is a member.

This allergy apart, camomile's reputation as an all-round cure remains high. It is useful as a natural insecticide – sponge any exposed parts of the body with water in which you have infused the dried flowers and no insect will want to come near you – while toothache, menstrual cramps, nervousness, loss of appetite, nausea, vomiting, headache, indigestion, earache and nappy rash can all be eased by it. In Britain the dried flowers should be easy to find in any natural food shop; visit a market in the Middle East and you might still find them being sold from giant barrels.

The medicinal properties are contained in the central yellow disc, and the double-flowered variety, in which this disc is smaller, is the one to use. Dr Thornton offers a terrible warning against the results of using the single variety over an extended period: 'the stomach, too much braced by a long-continued use of chamomile tea, loses irrecoverably its tone, and becomes a truly afflicting evil arising from imprudent use of the tonic'. Worrying.

I can vouch for the effects of camomile as a reducer of nausea. In the years when I lived in Corfu for much of the time, my annual dread was the Easter Day feast at which the foreigner of the village was hospitably invited to work her way through a massive plate of macaroni, followed by at least three huge and steaming platters of roast lamb. Perhaps I'm over-sensitive, but it took only a brief prior glimpse of the pale corpse revolving on the spit for my stomach to give an ominous heave. Camomile tea was the remedy provided, and the ladies of the village firmly dosed me with it until my appetite returned. And it always did.

# CELANDINE
## *Chelidonium majus*

THE ODDITY OF the lesser and greater celandine is that the colour of their flowers apart, they have nothing to do with one another. They don't even belong to the same species. The plump leafy plant shown in the drawing is *Chelidonium majus*, the greater celandine or wartweed; the root and tuber cluster resembling a broom handle festooned with potatoes belongs to *Ranunculus ficaria*, also known as figwort, pilewort and lesser celandine. The first belongs to the poppy family, the other to that of the buttercup.

The Ranunculaceae derive their name from the Latin diminutive for *rana*, a frog, through their fondness for marshy places. Not that this has ever constrained them. The high fields around our home were thick with buttercups when I was a child, and the lesser celandine is often seen on mountain slopes in Wales. Wordsworth's two famous poems about the celandine celebrate the habit children living near Grasmere had of making plots of flowers in springtime and festooning them with the lesser celandine's glossy yellow petals. Unfortunately, Grasmere's monument to Wordsworth proudly displays the wrong form.

The eighteenth-century clergyman and naturalist

Gilbert White carefully recorded the first appearance of the lesser celandine at Selborne on 21 February. Its obliging show of colour in a dull season
has given it the name of the spring messenger, but
confusion over the names of the two celandines sets
in when we look beyond the fact that the Celtic
name was *grian*, meaning sun, to the word from
which 'celandine' itself is derived. *Chelidon* is
Greek for swallow, and the greater celandine is
sometimes called swallow-wort, which may simply
refer to the fact that it flowers when the swallows
return at the end of the winter. An odder myth gave
rise to its reputation as an herbal eye remedy.
Culpeper tells us that 'if you put out the eyes of
young swallows when they are in the nest, the old
ones will recover their eyes again with this herb'.
Never mind why anyone would want to do anything so vicious: don't believe it. The acid in the
leaves is more likely to damage eyes than cure them.

Celandine's ubiquitous presence in Oxford is
ascribed to the city's patron saint, Frideswide.
Having punished an unwanted suitor by blinding
him, Frideswide then used the celandine-surrounded
well of Binsey to cure him. The city took note and
imported Binsey celandine, and it has thrived in
Oxford's gardens ever since.

Lesser celandine earned the name pilewort from
the striking resemblance of its bulbous roots and
tubers to haemorrhoids. To look like was to cure,
according to the Doctrine of Signatures: strangely,
no better cure for piles has been found in natural
medicine. Discomfort can be eased with an ointment made from the macerated leaves and roots,
strained and mixed with almond oil, witch hazel,
marigold, and a drop of benzoin as a preservative.

Culpeper seems to have confused the two forms
of celandine in recommending *Ranunculus ficaria* as
a cure for both piles and warts: it is *Chelidonium*

*majus* which is the wonder wart cure (only comfrey and feverfew have a reputation to match it). Squeeze a little of the juice from a leaf onto the wart three times a day and it should disappear. Beware of taking it internally, however, and don't overdo the juice, which is acid: medieval beggars used it to raise pitiable blisters on their skins (and later treated them with soothing mullein leaves).

William Copland, printer of the sixteenth-century compilation *The boke of secretes*, thought highly of celandine, although it is not certain which sort he had in mind. 'If any man shal have this herbe with ye harte of a Molle [mole],' he wrote, 'he shall overcome all his enemies.' It could, moreover, cause a dying man to sing. Or so he claimed.

# CHERVIL
## *Anthriscus cerefolium*

Rousseau, tired of luxury, of elegant women and long, elaborate meals, thought nothing would be more delightful than to visit the home of a simple housewife and eat a chervil-scented omelette. You wouldn't catch an English eighteenth-century writer saying that; chervil has always been more respected in France, where it is an essential ingredient of *fines herbes* and frequently used to enhance the flavour of egg dishes, fish, and mushroom-based sauces.

Chervil derives its botanical name from the Greek *chairophyllon* meaning happy or delightful leaf. This may explain its slightly mysterious appearance in Aristophanes's oldest extant play, *The Acharnaians*. Here Mr Just City, keen to disguise himself as a beggar for reasons which would take too long to explain, enlists the help of his friend Euripides. The celebrated dramatist is surprisingly willing to hand over all the props Mr Just City needs, but draws the line at giving him the chervil which was left to him in his mother's will.

Were the ancient Greeks in the habit of bequeathing chervil in their wills? Did they endow it with some special attribute, lost to us today? It seems likely that Aristophanes and his audience were sharing a reference which has since lost its significance for us.

Pliny praised chervil as a warmer of 'the cold stomach of the aged', later herbalists as a cure for hiccoughs when infused in vinegar, and as a reducer of phlegm when drunk as a tea. Culpeper noted its value as a poultice to soothe inflamed joints; today, chervil is drunk as a tisane to purify the blood, and dabbed on the skin to soothe and clear it.

The leaves make a handy substitute for parsley in cases of bad breath, and as an added bonus the herb is said to increase sexual appetite. (Don't get too excited: the lust, according to John Gerard, results from chervil's propensity to provoke 'windiness'.) Chervil is also one of several herbs with an impressive reputation for lifting depression, sharing the honours here with comfrey, ginseng, lemon balm, milk thistle and St John's wort.

It is surprising that chervil is not more popular in Britain and America, for it is an attractive herb and not hard to grow. The seeds, if scattered in a shady spot, will germinate easily, producing a pretty plant with fernlike leaves and delicate flowers. A hardy annual, it turns pink and then red towards the end of its life, adding colour at a time when it is most welcome.

The Romans introduced chervil to the French, but its popularity in French cooking seems to have had much to do with the need to enliven the dull taste of Lenten food. It has the unusual property of adding a delicate taste of its own while at the same time enhancing the flavour of any other herb in the dish. The tradition of drinking chervil soup on Holy Thursday arises from the alleged similarity between the taste of chervil and that of myrrh, one of the gifts brought to the Bethlehem stable, hence it has acquired the symbolism of new life and hope.

Chervil is particularly good in scrambled or coddled eggs, omelettes and seafood. One of the most delicious ways I have tasted it was mixed with savory to enhance eggs lightly poached in cream. Chervil and cream were made for each other – but so were chervil and prawns, chervil and lobster, chervil and crab, chervil and mushrooms...

# CHICKWEED
*Stellaria media*

TOO WELL-KNOWN TO need description, in the opinion of Nicholas Culpeper, chickweed is 'a fine soft pleasing herb under the dominion of the Moon'. We know it best as a favourite of caged birds, a welcome alternative to groundsel and one which keeps its leaves throughout winter. *Stellaria media* – translated simply into starweed in America – is chickweed's official name, but *morsus gallinae* (medieval Latin for hen's bite), *vogelmiere* (German for birdweed) and *herbe à l'oiseau* all stress its value to hungry chicks rather than the tiny white flowers which can give it the look of an earthbound Milky Way in miniature.

The best news about chickweed for humans is that it is a formidable fat-buster. Ask any stockist of herbal remedies to suggest a quick way of losing weight and you'll probably be offered a course of chickweed-based capsules, rich in vitamins B and C and with a proven effect on an underactive thyroid. To speed up the effects you can try drinking water in which chickweed has been boiled. It is good for the digestion – the only disadvantage is its distinctly unappetising taste.

David Hoffman's *Holistic Herbal* is warm in praise of chickweed as a cure for itchy skin, applied

externally as an infusion of marigold and chickweed diluted with distilled witch hazel (you can
buy witch hazel from any dispensing pharmacy). A
collection of East Anglian herbal remedies from the
last eighty years enthusiastically endorses chickweed as an eczema cure; turning back to John
Gerard's *Herbal*, we can see that there is nothing
new in this, since Gerard recommends an application of chickweed boiled in vinegar and salt as a
good cure for dry legs and hands. I'm less taken by
an ancient Welsh cure for swellings, made from
mallow, camomile, maidenhair fern, ground-ivy
and chickweed, all boiled up in old urine, 'the
stalest you can get'. It doesn't charm.

To relieve skin complaints, a homely poultice of
ground-ivy and chickweed sounds less objection-
able. Culpeper would like you to plaster bruised
chickweed leaves over your liver, to ease strain and
also to reduce redness of the face. Less appealingly
again, he suggests dripping its juice onto genital
sores – ouch! – and grows lyrical about its wonderful effect on boils. (If I wanted to play detective, I
would say that Culpeper must have suffered horri-
bly from boils: he never misses a chance to
commend a cure for them.) A poultice made with
fenugreek, chickweed and linseed will do the trick,
he claims. His favourite use of chickweed, however,
is as a cure for cramps. Boil a handful of it, he tells
us, together with a handful of dry crimson rose
petals, in a quart of 'muscadine' (muscadet?).
Reduce by a quarter, then boil the residue with a
quarter-pint of oil made from ... sheep's trotters.
Apply while keeping the affected area open and
dry, bind on some of the weed '(if you will) ...
and, with God's blessing, it will help it in three
times dressing'.

Speaking of sheep, they aren't keen on chickweed, and goats hate it, but pigs, horses, rabbits

and cows are all, like birds, grateful consumers. We too can eat it, either in a salad with dandelion leaves or as a vegetable, chopped and cooked with a knob of butter and chopped spring onions for ten minutes. Add a pinch of nutmeg or lemon before serving, and if anyone is rude enough to raise an eyebrow, tell them chickweed is thinning, ecologically sound, and good for coughs.

With such an unromantic name, it's not surprising that chickweed rates pretty low in literature. A few obvious references to cages decorated with chickweed apart, the best I can find is from Hans Christian Anderson's week of stories told by a strange man who visits a little boy's room at bedtime. The child is content to be told how the chickseed courted the chickweed or how the darning needle learned to stand straight, less so when his sinister visitor opens the window and shows where his twin brother, Death, rides fast across the sky.

Equally tangential is Dickens's reference to chickweed in *Oliver Twist*. Conkey Chickweed is a small-time crook, a 'licensed vittler' or pub-keeper living near Battlebridge (King's Cross) who stages a robbery of himself and then, with imprudent cunning, claims to have spotted the robber, a sinister gentleman with a patch over one eye who keeps sidling past his premises and then running away. His connection with the story of Oliver is minimal, and Mr Chickweed may or may not be the burglar for whom Oliver is mistaken just before his rescue from the Bow Street officers by Mrs Maylie and Mr Losberne.

# CHIVES
*Allium schoenoprasum*

CHIVES GOBBLE UP nitrogen, but this can be remedied by planting them near comfrey, which refuels the soil. The little mauve puff-ball flowers which appear among the frail, hollow stems in late spring make chives pretty enough to be grown as an edging plant, and they too can be eaten. Be warned, however, that the chive stems will become much sharper in taste after the appearance of the flowers, so if they are of interest to you only as a cooking herb, snip them regularly to prevent flowering.

Not all the herbs included in this book are delicious, but chives are among the few herbs which enhance food while doing your body good – although not your breath ('The man who carries chives on his breath, Is never going to be kissed to death', Martial wrote, almost as if intending it as a recommendation). As a member of the onion family, chives are like their relations in benefiting the stomach and kidneys while lowering blood pressure and breaking down indigestible fats in food. I have read of chives being used to ease coughs, and even to fight anaemia. Best-known, however, is their astonishing effectiveness as an appetite stimulant. A sprinkling of chives may be all that is needed to provoke the taste-buds when scrambled eggs by themselves are rejected, and anybody who has made potato salad both with and without chives will have been struck by the difference in the enthusiasm of its consumers.

The Latin *cepa*, onion, seems to have given us the name chive, and its introduction by the Romans to Britain is pleasantly commemorated by the fact that one of the few places where chives appear to grow wild is at Whin Sill Ridge in Northumberland, once a Roman camp close to Hadrian's Wall. This contradicts the usual assertion that chives were not known in Britain until the Middle Ages.

The sixteenth-century Flemish herbalist Rembert Dodoens' mention of the chive being known in France as *petit poureau* or *petit poireau* suggests that it was being used in cooking in the same way as leeks. Apothecaries of the Middle Ages also valued chives as a cure for melancholy and for protection against evil spirits.

The flowers are more delicate in taste than the stems. You can add them to salads, or steep one and a half ounces of petals in a quart of sunflower oil for a couple of weeks, long enough to produce a flavoured salad oil, faintly lilac-tinted. To be most beneficial to health the stems should be eaten within an hour or two of being cut; the best way to preserve them is to snip them into an ice tray filled with water, then store the resulting chive cubes in freezer bags.

An unusually pretty salad can be made by mixing torn young lettuce leaves with a cup each of nasturtium and chive flowers, sprinkled with black pepper and tossed in a simple oil-and-vinegar dressing. Chopped chives and parsley with a couple of garlic cloves and a mixture of cream cheese and plain yogurt make a dip which is further improved by the addition of plenty of freshly ground black pepper. Keep the made-up mixture in the fridge for a few hours to develop the flavour. It's a nice dip for celery and carrot sticks. More yogurt will thin the mixture, more cheese will bulk it out.

And if anyone thinks chives are visually boring, Van Gogh's glorious 1887 painting of a flowerpot filled with them should end the discussion.

# COLT'S-FOOT
## Tussilago farfara

COLT'S-FOOT WAS ONE of the medicinal plants taken to the New World by British settlers. It was one of the most useful and best-known household remedies for every kind of bronchial condition, as its botanical name, *Tussilago*, indicates. So formidable was its reputation that the flowers were painted as a trade sign on apothecaries' shops in pre-Revolutionary Paris.

Why 'colt's-foot'? For the same reason that it is also known as horse-hoof, bull's-foot, ass's-foot: the broad, sea-green leaves bear a striking resemblance in shape to small hooves. The silky fluff which follows the yellow flowers is valued by goldfinches as a lining for nests and was once gathered to stuff mattresses and pillows in the Scottish Highlands: the time involved must surely have been phenomenal. The undersides of the leaves are thickly felted, and in Britain and throughout Europe, before the invention of the match, were wrapped in saltpetre-dipped rag for use as tinder.

Silas Marner is remembered chiefly as the miser of Raveloe in George Eliot's novel of 1861, but Eliot also discloses that he had been trained as a herbalist by his mother, and that he enjoyed his knowledge and his work. It was only when piety persuaded him that herbs must be blessed by prayers, and then that prayers alone should suffice to cure the sick, that Silas renounced his daily strolls in search of foxglove and dandelion and colt's-foot, and cured no more invalids. Eliot's low opinion of conventional religion is clear: a less pious man, she obliges her readers to conclude, would have been more useful to his fellows.

*Bechion* to the Greeks and *tussilago* to the Romans, colt's-foot has since acquired a host of other names. The-son-before-the-father refers to the fact that the small yellow flower, shaped like an elegant candle-snuffer, appears at the end of February, well before the leaves, which last until late summer; coughwort, cleats and tushylucky (a Scots name, and my favourite) all allude to its merits as a suppressant.

Pliny recommended inhaling the smoke of colt's-foot leaves over a fire of cypress wood. Gerard, who also calls its fole-foot, noted the oddity of the flowers preceding the leaves and wondered, a little smugly, that Pliny should have failed to remark upon this eccentric aspect of the plant. It 'groweth of itself neere unto Springs, and on the brinks of brookes and rivers,' Gerard reported, 'in wet furrows, by ditches sides, and in other moist and watery places neere unto the sea, almost everywhere.' The leaves, when pounded with honey, were believed by him to be a sure cure for inflammation. Dr Robert Thornton – an expert on small-pox inoculation, and the brains behind Britain's greatest book of flower-paintings, the astonishing *Temple of Flora* (1799–1807) – was unsurprisingly patronising about such a homely and unpaintable plant. It was, he noted in one of his many medical works, sometimes made into a form of tea, much enjoyed by 'the common people'. In his *Domestic Medicine* (1791) the less fastidious Scotsman

Dr Buchan recommended an infusion of wild poppy and colt's-foot leaves for coughs, while his cure for aching legs consisted of a poultice of colt's-foot leaves seethed in the milk of a cow of one colour, mixed with oat groats and 'May butter', whatever that may have been.

On the list of herbs which were to have been outlawed by European Union rules in the ultra-bureaucratic 1990s (it has since been completely banned in Germany), colt's-foot remains in favour with herbalists as a cure for coughs, along with white horehound and elecampane. One reputable author, Stephen Fulder, recommends combining it with licorice and ginkgo to maximise the effect. Another, David Hoffmann, suggests a tisane of equal parts of colt's-foot, mullein and licorice.

Still known in some parts of Somerset as the 'baccy plant', colt's-foot's history as the chief ingredient of herbal tobacco dates back to the time of Dioscorides. Linnaeus, travelling through Sweden in the eighteenth century, noticed people smoking it in just the way they did in England. It is conceivable – just – that the pains tobacco companies took in the early twentieth century to advertise some of the harshest cigarettes as a cure for sore throats were distantly connected to the fact that colt's-foot was smoked for precisely this reason.

To prepare colt's-foot for smoking, gather the leaves only and chop them small before drying. If you plan to include the flowers, make sure that they are not yet fully formed. To $3\frac{1}{2}$ ounces of colt's-foot add $\frac{1}{2}$ ounce each of eyebright, buckbean, betony, rosemary, wild thyme, lavender and camomile flowers. These ingredients can be mixed in varying proportions, so long as eyebright is always included and the amount of colt's-foot equals the total weight of the other ingredients. Keep dry in a tin or sealed plastic bag.

The roots of colt's-foot should never be taken internally, and the use of the leaves and flowers as a remedy should always be discontinued after a month. Colt's-foot is unsuitable for use in pregnancy. Drunk as a hot tea early in the morning, it is reported to be soothing to sufferers from emphysema. Ironic, really, given the smoking connection.

# COMFREY
## *Symphytum officinale*

I WISH I could have swapped my unexciting school botany teacher for Aristotle, a man observant enough to discover that the greenfinch in spring lays a blanket of comfrey on an under-nest of hair and wool (for more interesting nature notes, dip into his glorious *The History of Animals*).

Comfrey is not fussy about its habitat, but John Gerard noted that 'it joyeth in watery ditches, in fat and fruitful meadows'. No plant has a wider range of popular names, or more soundly-established properties. 'Comfrey' derives from *conferva*, in medieval Latin *confirma*, referring to the plant's reputation for healing broken bones. Pliny recommended comfrey, and medieval herbalists called it bone-set and kept jars of the root, lifted and grated in spring. Bruisewort and knitbone indicate the same use, while church bells alludes to the drooping clusters of cream, pinkish-purple and white or blue flowers. So, less prettily, does ass-ear – but what about Abraham, Isaac and Joseph, pigweed and gooseberry pie?

Gooseberries and comfrey don't sound a promising mix, but you can eat the stalks, blanched beneath an upturned flower pot, like skinny asparagus. Enthusiasts steam the young leaves like spinach, as a vegetable, and add a couple to the juicer when preparing a vegetable cocktail. One rather uninviting receipt for serving the leaves, lightly fried in batter, as a first course, suggests brightly that their strange appearance will be a talking-point: most guests would probably rather sit quiet over smoked salmon. Comfrey wine is a waste of time and effort, and I've yet to meet anybody who's made chutney from the roots, although it can be done. Comfrey coffee, if you're feeling masochistic, is also made from the roots.

Curing, not cooking, is what comfrey is good for. Its almost legendary power is due to the presence of allantoin in the roots (allantoin is the miracle ingredient in Clearasil's spot-blitzing face cleanser). As a tea, it has been used for everything from bronchitis to haemorrhages; the wives of crusaders sent them off with a tightly-sealed jar packed with the leaves, which eventually turned into an oily brew that could be rubbed on wounds, and worked. As late as the beginning of the twentieth century, Yorkshire miners used comfrey for the aptly-named 'beet knee' acquired by crawling along narrow seams. A poultice of hot comfrey leaves was guaranteed to bring the swelling down in twenty-four hours. Less plausibly, a hot plaster of chopped leaves is alleged to encourage hair-growth (first, ask yourself why, if it works, it hasn't been marketed). To prepare a poultice, strain the simmered leaves, and place a bandage over the application. At the very least, it will soothe an injury.

Manure is not a romantic topic, but do not overlook comfrey when preparing it. Wet comfrey leaves stuffed into a plastic carrier bag and left to rot will eventually produce a powerful liquid nutrient for tomato plants (dilute before application). You don't even have to go to this much trouble: simply digging a few spent leaves taken from the edge of a comfrey clump into the earth should do the trick. But before adding comfrey's cream, blue, rose-pink or purple flowers to your garden border, remember that you'll never be rid of it – comfrey springs up from every particle of severed root faster than soldiers from the field Jason dutifully scattered with dragons' teeth.

Anyone in doubt of comfrey's miraculous powers of healing might be converted by this story, told in Richard Mabey's splendid *Flora Britannica*. One of his correspondents, a doctor, told him of a patient who failed to respond to every kind of medical dressing for the wound left in his leg following a coronary artery bypass. The wound only healed after the application of a dressing soaked in an infusion of comfrey gathered from the proud patient's own garden. Convinced? If not, what about the Twickenham lock-keeper who lived in agony for two months after a broken finger was improperly set? The local doctor told him to take a piece of comfrey root, soften it and wrap it around his finger. Four days later, the finger was as good as new.

One last merit of comfrey: the prickly variety which bears a blue flower is said to be both a certain preventative and a cure of foot-and-mouth disease.

# CORIANDER
## *Coriandrum sativum*

CORIANDER ARRIVED IN England with the Romans and later became a stalwart of monastery gardens, from which the herb spread to the waste places and riverbanks which have become its typical habitat. Commonly used today in the kitchen, coriander was originally valued for its medicinal uses in stimulating the appetite, calming colicky babies and soothing the stomach. To try its effects as a tisane, pour boiling water over a teaspoon of the bruised seeds.

Coriander was always comparatively cheap. In 1254 it cost fourpence a pound and cloves fourteen shillings – forty-two times as much. Sir Hugh Platt commended it for making sweets in his *Delights for Ladies* (1609): 'A quarter pound of coriander seeds and three pounds of sugar will make great, huge and big comfrets,' he told his readers. Eighteenth-century distillers used coriander as well as juniper to flavour the gin in which the poor drowned their sorrows, and it acquired new popularity as an ingredient of the delicate curries introduced by families connected with the East India Company. Later, in the *Just So Stories*, Rudyard Kipling pictured the cave-dwellers in 'The Cat that walked by Himself' feasting on wild sheep flavoured with wild garlic and pepper and wild duck stuffed with wild rice and fenugreek and coriander.

Pliny named coriander from the word *koris*, a kind of bug – a reference to its foetid smell – and knew that the best form came from Egypt: he believed that the Israelites learned to respect its medicinal usefulness during their Captivity. William Turner, writing during the sixteenth century, thought coriander cakes, made with barley meal, were a good protection against the disease he called 'Saint Antonyes fyre' (erysipelas, according to one later herbalist). Gerard was silent about the herb's unpleasant bed-buggy smell, which only becomes tolerable and even rather delicious at the height of summer, and merely thought it 'very striking'. The smell the plant exudes from late spring until August makes it an uninviting member of the kitchen garden tribe, pretty though its foliage and white flowers look from a distance.

The seeds of coriander – strictly-speaking, they are its fruit – are delicious in potato salad and shepherd's pie, and are sometimes used like caraway, to flavour bread. Curry, however, remains its main home, and this curry sauce will keep in the fridge for up to four days.

Finely chop a bunch of coriander leaves with 2 tablespoons of cumin and a large pinch of cinnamon, then whizz in blender, slowly adding 4 ounces of olive oil, 2–3 tablespoons of wine vinegar and a generous pinch of sugar. Let stand for five minutes, then bottle.

An old recipe for Lucknow curry powder, quoted by Mrs Grieve, says: 'Have the best ingredients' (including an ounce of coriander seed) 'powdered at the druggist's into a fine powder and sent home in different papers.' Life could be very easy for the nineteenth-century shopper.

# DANDELION
*Taraxacum officinale*

JOHN GERARD COMPARED the dandelion to chicory ('succorie') and noted that it thrived especially in gardens 'and highe ways much troden'. Culpeper used it to make a pointed comparison between English physicians and their expensive cures and the doctors in France and Holland, where, he observed, no secret was made of the usefulness of the dandelion as an internal cleanser and purifier: 'if you look a little further,' he added, 'you may see plainly without a pair of spectacles, that foreign physicians are not selfish as ours.' No wonder the physicians of England detested him for his candour. Well into the late twentieth century, dandelion has been used to make a tea for indigestion, its leaves have been recommended as a cure for eczema, and the juice pressed from its roots as a treatment for nausea.

The French name *dents-de-lion* probably alludes to the long ragged leaves; less prettily, it has also been called swine's snout. Another old name, priest's crown, describes the bald disc left after the white puffball of seeds has blown away. In 1503 Dürer included a dandelion in his extraordinary grasshopper's-eye-view of a meadow; Walt Whitman was misty-eyed enough to write a poem to 'The First

Dandelion'; and Darwin admired the ingenuity of its featherlight 'clock', which can float over occupied soil and deftly parachute its plumed seeds on to the nearest bare patch.

Darwin saw a parachute. Shakespeare saw a broom-head, and used the dandelion's short life and ghostly end for one of his most haunting images: 'Golden lads and girls all must, As chimney sweepers, come to dust.'

The inelegant 'piss-a-bed' or *pissenlit* reveals the dandelion's formidable power as a diuretic, but eighteenth-century squires were ready to risk a wet bed because of its reputation as a gout cure. When it wasn't easy to grow lettuce in winter, dandelions appeared for afternoon tea, in sandwiches. The young leaves make a delicious salad – not unlike rocket, but a little more bitter – tossed with lots of garlic, chopped tarragon, chervil and black olives.

Sugary, black and cheap, bottled Dandelion & Burdock once sold almost as well as aniseed balls in the local sweet shop. Laurie Lee's autobiography tells us that dandelion wine was the preferred drink in his village. Laced with sliced ginger and fermented with yeast spread on a piece of toast, it's alleged to be delicious and potent (Mrs Grieve's *Herbal* of 1931 gives a detailed recipe). The roots of dandelion, simmered and strained, are a wart cure, while the leaves obligingly double as both diuretic and tonic when dried and steeped in boiling water for a tisane, and as a clarifying face mask when fresh leaves are briefly simmered, then drained, cooled and spread on the skin. Anyone who suggests you lift dandelion roots in autumn to roast and grind for coffee deserves to be given a bag of the results for their next Christmas present.

# DILL

## *Anethum graveolens*

MEDICINALLY, DILL'S HISTORY can be traced back to tablets in Egyptian tombs. But it also has a history as a magical herb: dill, along with yarrow, trefoil, verbena, rue and roses, is connected with the old and now neglected festival of Midsummer Eve.

June 23rd is one of the dates in the calendar on which pagan and Christian traditions become inextricably intertwined. Christians don't, in principle, have any truck with witchcraft, but June 24th has been St John's day for as long as anybody can remember, and the St John's fires lit in its honour the night before were regarded as a protection against sorcery, as were the herbs which were gathered to safeguard the homes of revellers. Did John have a more ancient, pagan history? Should we look harder at the fact that he is often carved in wood, and connect that with the way his day was celebrated with enormous bonfires? After all, they could scarcely be required for light or heat, on the longest day of the warmest season of the year.

Edmund Spenser relates how Glauce, the aged hag who looks after beautiful Britomart in *The Faerie Queen*, adds dill to the disgusting concoction with which she tries to calm Britomart's passion for a portly knight whose face she has seen in a magical mirror. Dill goes into Glauce's pot, along with rue, calamint, camphor flowers, colt's-foot, milk, blood and hair. All to no avail, for Britomart 'still did wayste, and still did wayle'.

*Anethon* is the Greek name for the herb, sometimes inaccurately translated as anise or aniseed. The word 'dill' is usually traced to the Old Norse *dilla*, meaning lull or soothe, an accurate description of its main medicinal use. Gripe water, the standard treatment for colic in babies, is produced from dill; a home brew can be made by soaking two teaspoons of crushed seeds in a cup of boiling water for ten minutes, to be given, diluted, in single-teaspoon doses to children under the age of two (a mixture made from a combination of dill and fennel seeds is also often recommended for babies). Adult sufferers can drink three teacups of the infusion a day. Chewed raw, the seeds are a remedy for bad breath and a strengthener of brittle nails; ground, they may make a spicy salt substitute; and the whole plant is said to stimulate the appetite if placed near the dining area.

In early times dill was sufficiently valued to feature in trade, and the Talmud, the Jewish book of law, reveals that it was subject to a tithe, another indication of its worth. Herbalists of the Middle Ages used dill as a panacea for their ills; by the time of Queen Elizabeth I it had begun to be esteemed as an enhancer of fish and vegetable dishes. One Elizabethan receipt suggests steaming spinach with sliced shallots and dill and serving it with a squeeze of lemon juice.

The history of dill pickles is almost equally venerable. In the days before refrigeration vegetables were frequently preserved in vinegar, and the unusually powerful bacteria-inhibiting preservatives contained in dill brought extra protection to the pickling process. I haven't been able to put a date on the discovery of the dill cucumber, but Charles I was a king who liked his pickles.

Nicholas Culpeper recommended dill as 'a gallant expeller of wind, and provoker of the terms'. Hiccough sufferers were urged to sniff a cloth which had been dipped in a pan of wine boiled up with dill seeds, while a dill bath was Culpeper's cure for 'women that are troubled with the pains and windiness of the mother, if they sit therein.'

Gardeners warn that dill should never be planted near fennel or angelica (because of the likelihood of cross-pollination). One plant should produce enough leaves for kitchen use and the seeds, gathered in summer, are most easily separated by rubbing the hollow stalk between your hands inside a large plastic bag.

Insomniacs might like to try an infusion of two parts dill seed and two parts anise seed to one part camomile flowers, steeped in boiling water and drunk, sweetened with honey, just before going to bed.

Dill can of course be used in a wide variety of dishes, but this seventeenth-century sauce is especially good with fish and vegetables.

| | |
|---|---|
| 1½ tbsps butter | 1½ tbsps flour |
| 1½ cups of stock (you can use a cube) | |
| 2 tbsps chopped dill | ½ tbsp sugar |
| ½ tsp lemon juice | 1 egg yolk |

Melt the butter, blend in the flour, then add the hot stock and the rest of the ingredients, except for the egg. Cool the mixture a little and stir in the yolk. Whisk and serve.

# ELECAMPANE
## *Inula helenium*

A'ROBUST AND stately plant' in Culpeper's description, elecampane has big ragged leaves and bright yellow flowers which look like a cross between small sunflowers and overgrown daisies. Sadly, it isn't easy to find nowadays, although a contributor to Richard Mabey's *Flora Britannica* names two flourishing sites in Shropshire. Given its striking appearance and its medicinal value, perhaps a sterner effort should be made to cultivate it.

A favourite with the Romans, elecampane takes its botanical name of *Inula helenium* from the pretty myth that Helen filled her hands with its flowers just before Paris carried her off from Greece to Troy. Another story tells of the plant springing from the ground she watered with her tears.

Lucretius must have liked elecampane. Studying atomic forms as elements in *The Nature of Things*, he classified it with wine as one of the elements which tend to 'tickle rather than to wound the sense And of which sort is the salt tartar of wine And flavours of the gummed elecampane.' He was probably thinking of the root which, when broken, has a faint smell of violets; the longer it is kept in a dry place, the sweeter the taste becomes.

Horace was another fan. His eighth Satire

describes a delicate sauce made with the boiled root, and recommends turnips and 'Enulas' as the perfect antidote to a heavy Roman dinner. Pliny, another enthusiast, thought that chewing the root was good for the gums, with the added benefit of helping the digestion and raising the spirits.

By early medieval times elecampane was firmly established in England as a good thing. Gerard, in his *Herbal*, was lovingly specific in his directions as to where it could be found: 'It groweth in medowes that are fat and fruitfull...' he wrote; 'it groweth plentifully in the fields on the left hand as you go from Dunstable to Puddle Hill; also in an orchard as you go from Colebrook to Ditton ferry, which is the way to Windsor' – a walk which in his view would be well worth the trouble, for elecampane 'is marvellous good for many things. It is good for shortnesse of breath, and an old cough, and for such as cannot breathe unless they hold their neckes upright.' Culpeper, as usual, went further in his claims, offering elecampane root for consumption, bronchial trouble, digestion, protection from the plague, and as an antidote to poison. The roots and leaves, when beaten and mixed with new ale, would do wonders for the eyesight, he told his readers, while a water distilled from the leaves and roots would clear blemishes and heal 'all sorts of filthy putrid old sores'. As a keen amateur astrologer, he also felt it important to state that elecampane grows under the dominion of Mercury.

Medieval housewives, who also knew it as scabwort and elfdock, threw elecampane roots on glowing embers to scent their rooms. By the nineteenth century, elecampane's main use was for cough sweets and – this on the Continent, rather than in England – as a flavouring for confectionery. English travellers would suck on a piece of root when travelling by rivers, to keep away the diseases thought to be carried on the stink of bad water. According to Mrs Grieve, elecampane root was also used in the preparation of absinthe, as well as for making a rich blue dye, when crushed with whortleberries. Monks, who can usually be relied on to brew a potent cordial, infused it with sugar and currants in white port.

For optimum medicinal value the roots of elecampane should be taken from plants not more than three years old and harvested in autumn, when the leaves have wilted. For coughs and asthma, boil 20 grams of dried root with 5 grams each of ginseng and liquorice root, and drink three times a day. If you feel tempted to grow it, elecampane looks handsome at the back of a decorative vegetable border along with globe artichokes and mullein, flowering from June to August.

# EYEBRIGHT
*Euphrasia nemorosa*

I T'S SURPRISING, GIVEN the number of lines poets
have devoted to eyes, that so few have a kind
word to spare for a herb which has never lost its
reputation as an ocular remedy. Small, with stalk-
less paired leaves, the eyebright would be easy to
miss were it not for the little flower with its distinctive lavender streaking on white petals and, in its
centre, a blotch of yellow bright as egg yolk.

Eyebright is a safer option than the belladonna
once so notoriously popular with vain ladies, used
to enhance their eyes by dilating the pupils. The
discovery of its properties seems to have had much
to do with the dubious Doctrine of Signatures:
since the lines of purple which stripe the white
flowers suggest a bloodshot eye, it was conjectured
that eyebright might be just the thing for a cure.
And so it proved. By the early fourteenth century,
Arnoldus Villanovanus had devoted a whole book
to the merits of eyebright; Matthaeus Sylvaticus,
physician to the Gonzaga family of renaissance
Mantua, recommended it for all ocular disorders;
William Coles, the respected seventeenth-century
herbalist, liked it enough to repeat Nicholas
Culpeper's little joke that the spectacle makers
of England would be put out of business by a

thorough investigation into its uses. Growing fanci-
ful in his best-known book, *Adam in Eden*, Coles
played on the Greek name for a linnet to suggest
that these birds were the first to use eyebright –
euphrasia – to clear the sight of their fledglings.
When they passed their knowledge on to man, the
little plant was named in their honour.

Eyebright's old names, Christ's eyes, Christ's
sight, opthalmica and luminella, all point towards
its chief use. In France, its nickname is *casse-lunette*,
or breaker of spectacles. We might question
Arnoldus Villanovanus's assertion that eyebright
has actually restored the sight of the blind, but John
Gerard was convinced that the juice, when mixed
with a little white wine and dropped into the eyes –
don't! – would take away any 'darkness and
dimness'; Culpeper added a suggestion that, 'tunned
up with strong beer', it would improve the memory.

Should we mock the old herbalists? Eyebright's
case suggests this would be rash. The Weleda
company still produce an eyedrop made from its
juice, and users praise its soothing effect on eyes
irritated by pollution or excessive computer-work.
In books of country remedies collected over the
past fifty years eyebright takes its place alongside
an infusion made from the tiny blue flowers of
speedwell (veronica) as one of the best natural eye
lotions (cucumber juice also has an excellent press,
and swollen eyelids can be rapidly soothed by the
application of crushed watercress). The most
appealing remedy, a Victorian one, is to cover the
eyes with a handkerchief folded around a wet
mixture of camomile flowers, cornflowers and rose-
petals, boiled together for a minute. (Cornflowers
are intended, by the way, should you ever
encounter the bizarre suggestion that you lay a
compress of 'blue bottles' on your eyes.)

The botanical name *Euphrasia* links the plant to

one of the three graces. Agalia was splendour, Thalia was comfort, and Euphrosyne was the life-enhancing spirit of joy and gladness. Eyebright was her gift to mankind, hence *Euphrasia*, but this may also be another link with the linnet, whose song was thought to express joy.

Eyebright will grow quite happily in the garden, so long as it is in a patch of grass rather than in soil. Look for it beside cliff paths and on heathy areas, since it does well on chalky ground.

# FENNEL
*Foeniculum vulgare*

LIKE SO MANY other herbs, fennel was known for its medicinal qualities long before it became a staple of the kitchen. Sophocles related how Prometheus brought fire back from Olympus in a hollow fennel stalk. It may have been the original thyrsus, the curiously-topped stalk carried by Dionysius; late depictions certainly seem to show him carrying a fennel wand, and because of its profligate seeding habits it may have been seen as a symbol of fertility. But fennel is also reported to have grown wild in the fields around Marathon; the Ancient Greeks called it *marathon*, from *maraino*, to grow thin, and their athletes ate it when preparing for the Olympic Games because it gave strength without fattening them.

Longfellow thought fennel was given to gladiators to add to their relish for a battle, and that the man who won was crowned with a fennel wreath. Confirmation can be found in Demosthenes, whose great rhetorical work *Oration of the Crown* tells of victors and kings being crowned with fennel and, rather uncomfortably, poplar branches. Ophelia and her riverbank-bouquet of rue, rosemary, fennel and columbine offered to the dismayed courtiers of Elsinore suggest that Shakespeare may have been thinking of Virgil's pretty water-maid, who 'of narcissus-flower And fragrant fennel, composes her bouquet.'

The ancient Romans placed branches of fennel under bread when it was baking to add to the flavour, which sounds surprisingly close to modern Italian cuisine; they also knew it as a refreshing wash for sore eyes, and as an effective appetite suppressant. Charlemagne used it to curb his hunger on campaigns, and it was presumably for its usefulness on fast-days that it was such a staple of late medieval households: Edward I's retinue once consumed eight pounds of it during Lent. Fast-days must have been noisy – one medieval poet recommends fennel-seed, because in it

> This virtue shall you finde,
>
> Foorth of your lower parts to drive the wind.

Culpeper was a great fan of fennel, so familiar in the gardens of his day with its feathered stalk and umbrella of yellow flowers that 'it needs no description'. He did, however, list some of its merits. The root, long and forked (unlike the plump bulb of the Florentine *finocchio* we generally use in cooking), was praised for its ability to strengthen the liver, protect against dropsy and act as a diuretic. Boiled, the leaves and root were commended as a cure for obesity; the seeds, boiled in barley water, were thought to be good for nursing mothers. Fennel cooked with conger eel was a popular dish in the seventeenth century – and Culpeper, like the medieval rhymester, noted that eating it, in this or any other form, would be 'goode to break wind'.

Lovers of swallowtail butterflies may like to know that fennel is a favourite source of nourishment for their caterpillars; it should not, however, be planted close to dill, coriander, wormwood, tomatoes or dwarf green beans, on which it has an adverse effect. Medically, it has been found to be of some value in strengthening muscular tissue; breast-enhancing creams often contain both fennel and fenugreek, a natural source of oestrogen. It has kept its reputation as an eye-wash – boil the leaves in water and use the strained liquid – and as a digestive which will be familiar to frequenters of Indian restaurants.

Fennel needs no endorsement as a culinary herb. Delicious sautéed in strips with *petits pois*, baked with mackerel or added to tomato sauce, it is also an essential ingredient of the true Marseillaise *bouillabaisse* (our English fish soup, lacking spiny lobster, scorpion fish and a few other local treats, remains a poor relation of this gorgeous dish).

# FOXGLOVE
## *Digitalis purpurea*

WITCHES' GLOVES, FOLK'S glove, fairy thimbles, dead men's bells, bloody fingers: these are a few of the imaginative names we have given to one of the most handsome – and most deadly – plants in the herbal. Richard Mabey thinks the name might be a reference to the tawny colour of the high-summer landscape from which the foxglove thrusts up its bell-hung stalk, but nice idea though this is, foxgloves are more usually found thriving in the damp greenery of dells than in open fields.

The earliest known version is *foxes glofa*, in the Anglo Saxon *Leechdoms* of *c.* AD 1000, and a Norse legend suggests that the fox always gloves his paws before stealing out for a night of fun and slaughter in the hen roost or on the riverbank. It was first called *digitalis* only in the mid sixteenth century, when Leonard Fuchs latinised the German name *fingerhut* – 'finger-hat', a thimble.

Herbalists of the seventeenth century had no real sense of the foxglove's medicinal value, although Nicholas Culpeper noted that foxglove ointment made 'one of the best remedies for a scabby head that is', and John Gerard, writing a little earlier, had recommended foxglove tea to purge 'grosse and slimy flegme and naughty humours'.

It was as a cure for dropsy that foxglove rose to fame at the end of the eighteenth century. Dropsy, or hydrops, meaning water retention, was a hideous disease. Erasmus Darwin claimed to have been the first to discover digitalis's power to relieve it and also wrote a poem about it in his astonishing *The Botanic Garden* (1794–5): 'Pale Dropsy rears his bloated form, and pants . . . thirst consumes him mid circumfluent waves.' Luckily for the patient in this case, 'Divine Hygeia' hears his howl of pain and comes to the rescue, wearing 'bright Digitalis' dress and air'.

Foxglove leaves were already in use as a country cure for dropsy when Darwin wrote his poem, and one of his colleagues, Dr William Withering, had begun an intensive study of the plant in 1775. Experimenting with it on a flock of turkeys, he confirmed his suspicion that the herb in its natural state was lethal; administering it to the dropsy-sufferers among his Birmingham patients, he learnt to reduce and refine the dose. His book, *An Account of the Foxglove*, published in 1785, is a classic in medical history in which Withering meticulously recorded his case histories over ten years of research. Although they did not lead to an immediate revolution, his conclusions were almost all confirmed during the next hundred years. Withering was known to colleagues as a difficult character, but he deserves to be honoured as one of the fathers of modern medicine.

The value of digitalis as a heart medicine had been established; its dangerous use as a herb simple continued. In Covent Garden, at the time when Dr Robert Thornton published his popular *Herbal* (1810), people were still buying handfuls of foxglove leaves to use as a home cure for dropsy. Thornton himself saw no harm in reporting that he knew a coachman's daughter who took four cups of foxglove tea a day. His own interest in the plant's curative potential is indicated by the fact that he quoted letters from all the leading doctors of the day (Beddoes, Hunter, Darwin, Withering) endorsing its efficacy in treating not only dropsy but tuberculosis, hydrocephalus, epilepsy and palpitations.

One puzzle remains: why was it that John Gerard recommended the use of foxglove for those 'who have fallen from high places'? Did Gerard envisage such people poisoning themselves out of despair for all they had lost – or was the foxglove thought to possess some consolatory property? Gerard was intimate with the Elizabethan court: is this perhaps some sly topical reference, now lost on the modern reader?

The foxglove is not, under any circumstances, to be used for making herbal remedies at home. Valuable though digitalis is as a heart stimulant, it must be taken only under medical supervision. Bees love the foxglove, but no bird or animal will touch it. And neither should you.

# GARLIC
*Allium sativum*

Eaten, so we're told, by the slaves who built the Pyramids, garlic was fondly remembered by the Israelites as an Egyptian delicacy, along with fish, cucumber, melons and leeks. Hippocrates recommended it as a cure for boils; spots can be brought to a head by a dab of garlic juice. As a fairly dubious cure for baldness, you can try rubbing your head daily with mashed cloves.

Known since early times for its formidable antiseptic qualities, garlic sold at a shilling a pound during the First World War, when a dab of garlic on sphagnum moss was found to be one of the most effective germ-killers for use in the trenches. Montaigne, in his *Essays*, noted that garlic was used by country people as a cure-all, and 'poor man's treacle' – to distinguish it from the expensive 'Venice treacle' of which bay leaves were an ingredient – is one of its old names. Its medicinal as well as culinary properties caused the practical Romans to carry garlic from Italy to wherever in the Empire they could coax it to flourish. It is tremendously good for the circulation, and an infusion of crushed cloves in warm water or milk can also be used to reduce high blood pressure.

Anyone who has travelled in the East will know

that garlic has a venerable reputation as a preventative against cholera and typhoid, but it was from pure greed that on a visit to Goa I became addicted to the breakfast delicacy of toasted *nan* bread stuffed with about twenty cloves of garlic. For reasons I still fail to understand, this left no smell on the breath. Garlic can certainly make you sweat; perhaps the smell simply evaporates when the cloves are consumed in intense heat? Just a hint of the flavour can be given to salad by rubbing a wooden bowl with a peeled clove – Queen Victoria's cook, it is said, used to chew a clove and simply *breathe* over the royal lettuce. Aïoli, for those with stronger stomachs, is best made with fresh garlic pounded and beaten up with the yolk of an egg before slowly dripping in, beating as you go, the finest olive oil you can buy. Roasting the cloves in their skins in the juices around a joint of lamb is an easy and delicious way of adding a French touch to Sunday lunch.

There's a hint of nostalgia for his own childhood in Kipling's references to Kim as yearning for 'the saffron-tinted rice, garlic and onions' of the Indian bazaars. But Kipling knew of a much odder use: in *The Jungle Book*, Mowgli smears his skin with garlic before an encounter with the sinister 'Little People'. In case you haven't looked at Kipling's children's books recently, the 'Little People' are identified as 'the busy, furious, black wild black bees of India'. Mowgli evidently knew what he was about, since they flee from his small garlic-anointed person when he walks among them.

This brings us to garlic's use as an amulet without which no self-respecting vampire-slayer can go about his business. This notion derives from the superstitious belief that garlic's evil smell draws the impure to itself and thus protects the wearer. Dracula's local villagers were impressively well-informed in this respect: Jonathan Harker, on his way to visit the count, was presented with a crucifix, a sprig of mountain ash, a wild rose – and garlic. It wasn't, however, to ward off blood-suckers that crafty Hungarian jockeys used to fasten a sprig of garlic to the bridles of their horses, but to keep competitors away.

Finally, an unusual cure for 'the hooping or chin-cough' is given in Dr William Buchan's eighteenth-century family work, *Domestic Medicine*: garlic ointment, he wrote, is made 'by beating in a mortar garlic with an equal quantity of hogs' lard. With this the soles of the feet may be rubbed twice or thrice a day; but the best method is to spread it upon a rag, and apply it in the form of plaster.' This, according to Dr Buchan, is 'an exceeding good medicine'.

# HORSETAIL
*Equisetum arvense*

I F YOU WANT to see horsetail in an intriguing
setting, visit the old herb garret hidden away at
the top of a spiral staircase above St Thomas's
Church in Southwark, south-east London. This was
where the herbs most commonly used in the nearby
St Thomas's Hospital were dried and dispersed.
When the hospital was forced to move in 1862 as
a consequence of the development of Waterloo
Station and its incoming lines the garret fell into
disuse; it was only rediscovered in 1957. The herbs
you will see there today are those which would
have been most popular a hundred and forty years
ago: willowbark for stomach upsets, hops as a
soporific, marshmallow and colt's-foot for bronchial
coughs, comfrey and horsetail for healing wounds.

Horsetail's nicknames of shave grass, gunbright,
scouring rush and bottlebrush plant indicate its
most common function in the past: the scratchy
silica crystals it contains make it a wonderful cleaning and polishing agent. The Romans used horsetail
for their pots and pans, fletchers to polish the tips of
their arrows, woodcarvers like sandpaper. Medieval
housewives were so pleased with the shine it produced that they named it pewterwort. Dairymaids in
the nineteenth century used horsetail to scrub out

their wooden pails. Though long since replaced by manmade scourers, horsetail could still offer stiff competition – and it was apparently still being sold as a cleaner in Austrian markets in the 1950s.

The pleasing way the hollow stems can be pulled apart and put back together again in sections has earned it the modern popular name of Lego plant, but it's hard to verify whether horsetail was the inspiration behind the ubiquitous blocks. More certain is the intriguing fact that horsetail is descended from a giant of the Palaeozoic period (about four hundred million years ago). The Latin name, combining *equus*, horse, and *seta* or *saeta*, bristle, indicates that its resemblance to a horse's tail has always been considered striking, although nowadays we might be inclined to liken it to young asparagus, or a small, spiky Christmas tree.

If you fancy snake-charming, horsetail stems will provide you with a handy whistle which reptiles are said to find particularly alluring; horsetail stems can also be laid in a corner of the bedroom to increase fertility – or so the old books claim.

Horsetail has a solid medicinal reputation dating back to the Classical writers on herbs, Dioscorides and Galen. John Gerard quoted both as the sources for his own commendation of horsetail as being 'of so great and singular a virtue in healing of wounds' that it could cure ruptures and internal 'burstings'. The stems of *Equisetum arvense*, the field or common horsetail, are the ones you need to make tisanes and poultices. Gather them in June or July when they are green and dry them carefully to ensure that they keep their colour, then store in sealed containers. To make a tisane, soak 2 teaspoons of the dried and chopped stems in a cup of water for 10–15 minutes. Drunk up to six times a day, it can help with bronchitis or any form of urinary ailment, and helps to enrich the blood.

Mouth ulcers can be eased by holding the tea in the mouth for a minute; the mixture can also be dabbed on wounds, or on a cottonwool plug to stop a nose-bleed. It will also soothe puffy eyelids.

Because it's good for the circulation, horsetail tea will improve the quality of your nails and hair. An old-fashioned cure for chilblains was to thrash them with holly until they bled; you might prefer to ease the irritation by drinking horsetail tea or dabbing it onto the inflamed skin. Less usefully, perhaps, certain forms of horsetail store gold dust in their tissues – not enough to be worth gathering, but sufficient to suggest there is more to be found – and the Iroquois of North America knew that its presence indicated a water-supply. Gardeners who despair of eradicating it from their borders may be consoled to know that, mixed up in the proportions given for a tisane, horsetail makes a superb natural fungicide against rose mildew. It can even, it is alleged, be used to promote weight loss.

# HYSSOP
## *Hyssopus officinalis*

'PURGE ME WITH hyssop and I shall be clean,' churchgoers sing in the 51st Psalm, but few are likely to connect hyssop's ancient history as a cleansing herb with the fact that this is the moment when the priest may sprinkle the congregation with holy water.

Purists point out that *Hyssopus officionalis* was not indigenous to Israel, and that savory, caper or marjoram are more likely to have been the sacred *azaf* or *ezob* with which lepers rubbed themselves before making physical contact with others. Lew Wallace, author of *Ben Hur*, ignored this, placing 'scrubby hyssop' on the Hill of Calvary: in Wallace-speak, 'the old Aramaic Golgotha – in Latin, Calvaria; anglicised, Calvary; translated, The Skull.' Going back a bit, the Book of Exodus records Moses as having told the Jewish elders to mark their doorposts with hyssop dipped in lamb's blood so that the Lord would not mistake them for Egyptians as he went about his acts of vengeance. My favourite hyssop quotation, however, comes from Bulwer-Lytton's *Last Days of Pompeii* (1834). After a decadent feast, the guests wash their hands in hyssop water before watching a display of tight-rope dancing – just as if, the novelist adds, they were at Vauxhall Gardens or Astley's Circus.

Shrubby, vigorous and sun-loving, hyssop can be clipped into a hedge, or wedged into a chink in a wall, where the brilliant blue flowers of some forms make a particularly cheerful display. It is strongly aromatic, hence its early popularity as a strewing-herb, so that caution is needed when cooking with it – just a leaf or two will give a strong, minty scent to a salad or soup. Old-fashioned cookery books sometimes recommend it for pies and sausages, and the flowers can also be used.

Medicinally, hyssop has always been well spoken of. Gerard grew several varieties in his London garden and recommended it as a cordial with figs, water, honey and rue for 'the old cough'. Turner before him had written fondly of 'ye comen hysop that growethe in all parts of England'. Culpeper too was a fan, suggesting hyssop mixed with honey for asthma, with figs as a laxative, with wine for inflammations, and boiled with vinegar for toothache. A few drops of hyssop oil were his special cure for head lice.

Several herbals follow Culpeper's recommendation of a poultice of hyssop leaves for cuts and bruises; all say the leaves should be mixed with sugar, but not why. The botanist John Ray's *British Flora* (1670) has an impressive account of a man who cured himself within a few hours of both the pain and the appearance of a violent kick on the thigh from a horse, simply by bandaging boiled hyssop leaves over the injured area. It is also useful for applying to open cuts, and Victorian farmworkers, who often had to use rusty machinery, swore by hyssop leaves. It is sometimes said that hyssop's curative powers are linked to the fact that its leaves will grow the mould which produces penicillin, but they are not unique in that, and the amount of penicillin produced is hardly worth mentioning.

Hyssop distils into an oil strong enough to give you convulsions if taken internally, but you can add it to a pot pourri, pour a single drop into the bath, or apply it to the skin in a dilution of 10 drops to 20 ml of almond oil. You can also put hyssop in drawers to keep away ants and moths, and impress your friends by commenting on the flavour it gives to Chartreuse liqueur. Magicians will already know that it is ideal for the washing of ritual robes.

Hyssop's main reputation is as a cough cure, and it is often taken in combination with white horehound since they share the same properties. A receipt for a cough-curing tea which dates back almost to the time of Hippocrates is 2 teaspoons of the dried herb (the best tea is made with the flowers) to a large cup of boiling water, sweetened with sugar or honey.

No apiarist will need to be told how happy both bees and customers will be if hyssop grows near the hives. It will tempt cabbage butterflies away from their prey onto its own more alluring flowers, and is said to be beneficial to grape vines. Who would not want to grow hyssop in their garden, if only for the sake of its pretty flowers, which can be in bloom from June through to the end of September, depending on the variety.

# INDIAN HEMP
## *Cannabis sativa*

'MAKE THE MOST of the Indian hemp seed and sow it everywhere' – thus George Washington to his gardener at Mount Vernon in 1794. It's hard to imagine a modern political leader in the West being able to endorse the plant we know as cannabis with such candour.

Hemp pots have been found dating back to the time, over two thousand years ago, when the Emperor Sheng Nun of China recognised cannabis as giving relief from the symptoms of malaria. For centuries the long fibrous stems of the plant provided the world's main source of paper and the raw material for a strong and durable cloth. Today, clothes designers are rediscovering its value as a practical alternative to linen; in earlier times, hemp was used for ropes and for making sails (the word 'canvas' comes to us from the Dutch for cannabis).

The Chinese used hemp for making shoes, bowstrings and fishing nets; India's Ayurvedic physicians found it invaluable as an analgesic; hemp-seed, besides being a valuable nutrient and a remedy for dry skin conditions, produced the oil which Rudolph Diesel, in 1896, planned to utilise in the new form of fuel he had discovered and to which he gave his name. Hemp had already established itself on both sides of the Atlantic as a valuable crop, so valuable for rope manufacture that Henry VIII levied a fine on any farmer who refused to grow it (the seed was traditionally planted on Good Friday). In America, hemp was only displaced as the top commodity crop by the inexorable rise of cotton and tobacco.

A young Irish doctor working in Calcutta in the 1830s was the first Westerner to notice that cannabis was being used to alleviate a wide range of muscular conditions, easing epilepsy as effectively as rheumatism. Dr O'Shaughnessy's report was published in England, and attracted much interest: with an effective-to-lethal ratio of 40,000 to 1 (some modern painkillers have a 10 to 1 likelihood of damaging you through abuse or error) cannabis soon became widely used in England in the treatment of muscular problems. Queen Victoria gave it the royal stamp of approval when she began smoking cannabis cigarettes to ease menstrual cramps. It is not recorded whether she took hashish, produced from the resin of *Cannabis sativa* ssp. *indica*; Dr O'Shaughnessy's preference was for the milder ganja, made from the flowering heads of female plants. The Queen was no solitary enthusiast: cannabis was one of the three most-prescribed drugs during the last forty years of her reign. Only the discovery of the hypodermic syringe in the 1850s impaired its progress: hemp products are not water soluble, and cannot be injected.

Cannabis has been used as a recreational drug since its earliest days; many Moslems, prohibited from drinking alcohol, have found cannabis to serve the purpose just as well. In the West, cannabis began to 'swing' in the Prohibition era. Reefer songs celebrated the pleasures of puffing joints, whether you were a cop or a jazz musician. Problems began when cannabis-smoking Mexican migrants flooded northwards in search of work; they weren't welcome, and a dirty campaign was initiated to prove that their use of the drug made them violent and therefore dangerous. By the early 1930s posters were warning against 'The Devil's Weed with Roots in Hell': cannabis had replaced alcohol as Public Enemy Number One. The Marijuana Tax Act of 1937 imposed a mass of bureaucratic restrictions which discouraged doctors from prescribing it, and in 1941 the drug was struck out of the pharmaceutical lists. The anti-drug fervour of the 1960s led to a ban on the use of cannabis in the Western world which has not, at the time of writing, been lifted. In the United States, a federally supported farm in Mississippi produces, at considerable expense, enough cannabis to meet the needs of just eight patients annually selected for treatment. This is a small concession; in Britain, growing or selling cannabis can still earn you a formidable prison sentence.

This is regrettable. Used under supervision, cannabis has been shown to be of value in helping patients withdraw from the use of morphine and heroin (in these cases, the patients were treated with THC or tetrahydrocannabinol, the main psychoactive cannabinoid). It has been used effectively to help treat delirium tremens (this was one of O'Shaughnessy's discoveries), to reduce pain for cancer patients, to relieve depression and boost tranquillity. Given that research shows *Cannabis indica* may also be useful in treating Tourette's Syndrome and even Alzheimer's disease, maintaining its illegal status seems short-sighted.

# LAVENDER
## *Lavandula angustifolia*
## (syn. *officinalis*)

L AVENDER WAS ONE of the herbs Gulliver stuffed into his nostrils to keep out the unpleasant odour of his own kind after returning to Lisbon from his travels. Judith, preparing to seduce Holofernes before cutting his head off, anointed her skin with lavender – strange that her victim should have found a scent we usually associate with linen and old ladies so irresistibly aphrodisiac.

In Francis Bacon's imaginary garden of all the seasons lavender was awarded a place among the winter evergreens because he thought its misty colour would look handsome there. I like to think Bacon would be pleased to see how many modern custodians of great country-house gardens share his affection for the plant, although there is currently no sign of a revival of the pretty seventeenth-century Irish tradition of growing lavender lawns.

The Misses Steele, in Jane Austen's *Sense and Sensibility*, used lavender water to soothe Lady Middleton's squalling infant, but Nicholas Culpeper had warned against overuse of the pure 'Oil of Spike'. 'Spike' and 'nard', from the Greek *nardos* (after Naarda in Syria), are among the names given to lavender in old books; they refer to *Lavendula spica*, the species known as English lavender, with narrow leaves, which produces the strongest and least agreeable oil. This, Culpeper wrote, 'is of so fierce and piercing a quality, that it is cautiously to be used, some few drops being sufficient ... either for inward or outward griefs.' Dr Thornton, writing in 1810, recommended a warming cordial of lavender for 'hysteria, lowness and other nervous affections.' William Turner, two centuries earlier, had offered the charming idea of quilting lavender flowers into a close-fitting cap, to protect the wearer from disease and 'comfort the brain'. Can't you picture John Aubrey writing his gossip-filled 'Lives' in a little nightcap laced with lavender flowers?

The name lavender is thought to derive from the Latin *lavare*, by way of the Romans' use of it as a bath perfume, and the connection is still strong. Muslin bags of dried lavender can be dropped in the bath, or placed under the pillows the day before a bed is to be used; laid in drawers of wool socks or sweaters, lavender bags also keep out moths. Don't keep the same bags for more than a couple of years, as the moths are only deterred when the scent is strong. For a treat, try drying your laundry on lavender bushes, as legend tells us the Virgin Mary dried the baby Jesus's swaddling clothes.

Lavender tea (use $1\frac{1}{2}$ teaspoons of flowers to 8 oz water) is said to alleviate migraine and any form of nervous tension; old herbals recommend it as a relaxant during childbirth. Lavender water is good for the skin and the flowers, pinched until they release a little oil, will rid the fingertips of furtive smokers of the smell of nicotine. The oil, best bought from a commercial stockist, can be applied undiluted to bites and stings, slightly diluted in cases of scalds and sunburn, and heavily diluted (10 drops to a teacup of water) as a hair rinse to prevent – it won't get rid of them – lice. Children won't mind it, for the smell is quite pleasant.

Lavender came to England in the army kitbags of the Romans, who had faith in its power to soothe wounds; nurses in the First World War resorted to the same treatment, dabbing the oil on with wads of sphagnum moss.

My mother likes to pour a pot of ordinary runny honey into a saucepan, add a handful of freshly-picked lavender flowers and gently heat the mixture for ten minutes before straining. The result is delicious. You can make lavender vinegar almost as easily by putting a few sprigs of fresh lavender into a bottle of white wine vinegar and leaving it on a sunny windowsill for a fortnight. Lavender vinegar tastes strangely delicious sprinkled on fresh strawberries, and can also be used to spice up a savoury sauce or jelly.

The deep purple variety 'Hidcote' is the loveliest lavender to grow, but be sure you're buying the genuine article: the least pallor in the flowers indicates a poor relation. Lavender fans also love 'Munstead', slightly shorter and named for the house belonging to that lavender-fan and queen of the mauve and grey colour scheme, Gertrude Jekyll. But the lavender bush I have the greatest affection for grows on a north London street. Rampaging along beside a wall the length of a billiard table and standing at least four and a half feet high, it came back with a honeymoon couple from Grasse as a sprig in 1947 and smells sweetly enough to smother the sour after-wake of the lorries and delivery vans thundering past.

# LEMON BALM
## *Melissa officinalis*

L EMON BALM IS one of the few herbs about which
the Greeks have nothing to say, an odd omis-
sion given their fondness for honey and the fact
that *melissa* is the Greek for honey bee, and bees
love its little white flowers. 'They are delighted with
this herbe above all others,' John Gerard noted in
his *Herbal*, 'whereupon it hath been called apias-
trum for ... when they are straied away, they doe
find their way home again by it.' Medieval gardeners grew lemon balm around the plots where bee-
hives were kept, and some even smeared the insides
of the hives with the crushed petals to bring in a
lost or truant swarm.

In Gerard's day lemon balm was the most
popular of all the lemon-scented herbs, partly
because it is so hardy. Lemon verbena may be pret-
tier and still more delicious in scent, but is unlikely
to survive a very wet or cold winter, while one of
the many charms of lemon balm is that you don't
need to do a thing about it except ensure that it
doesn't run out of control. Once settled in, there's
no holding it. The Edwardians liked it planted in
broad bands in front of sweet Cicely and angelica
for an attractive contrast in heights – but there
were plenty of under-gardeners around to control

the borders in those days. You can enjoy lemon balm for its bee-pulling powers, or for the value of its leaves in the home: you can't, unfortunately, do both, because when it comes into flower, the leaves lose their potency.

'An essence of balm, given in canary wine every morning, will renew youth, strengthen the brain, relieve languishing nature and prevent baldness,' states the *London Dispensary*, published in 1691. Modern trichologists are reluctant to endorse claims that lemon balm can cure baldness, but in her herbal Maud Grieve mentions two venerable gentlemen who lived to 108 and 116, convinced that they owed their energy to starting each day with lemon-balm tea. There are plenty of reasons to follow their example; recent research suggests that lemon balm may be effective against backache, herpes and even Alzheimer's disease.

We get a glimpse of life in a Jacobean household from Culpeper's recommendation that a syrup made from the juice of lemon balm mixed with sugar 'be kept in every gentlewoman's house to relieve the weak stomachs and sick bodies of their poor and sickly neighbours'. In his day lemon balm was made into a hot poultice to ripen boils, while women in childbirth or in pain from menstruation were thought to benefit from the sedative powers of a warm bath infused with the leaves.

As a matter of taste rather than health, lemon balm leaves make a delicious alternative to borage in a chilled wine-cup or Pimm's; you can also try putting a sprig in a jug of dry white wine, or use it to flavour vinegar (it goes particularly well with a sprig of tarragon). In cooking, the leaves can be used in just about anything which requires a slightly lemony taste. A few chopped leaves will counteract the blandness of an orange mousse, and try a little in ice-cream, chilled soups and mayonnaise. You can also – and the result smells delicious – mimic the medieval housewife and rub it over unwaxed wooden furniture.

Intriguingly, lemon balm has an additional history as the chief ingredient of a fragrance which also served as a fairly lethal drink; like Benedictine and Chartreuse, it started life in a monastery garden. Eau des Carmes was invented in 1611 in a Carmelite monastery in Paris; the monks patented it and did quite nicely in sales until the suppression of the monastic orders in 1799. Some Carmelites from the monastery of Van Girard promptly formed a private company to make balm water and carried on doing so until the death of the last of the monks, Brother Paradise. More venal by nature than name, Brother Paradise had already taken a business partner, whose widow, a Madame Rozer, kept Eau des Carmes scent production going well into the 1860s, at which point eau-de-Cologne rose up in the popularity stakes and swamped its predecessor.

# LOVAGE
## *Levisticum officinale*

LOVAGE, THE MOST handsome member of the Umbelliferae family, with its large winged leaves and circular sprays of yellow flowers, has been a favourite of herbalists' gardens since at least the days when it was grown in monastery plots. In the doggerel verse of his *Five Hundred Points of Good Husbandry*, published in 1573, Thomas Tusser recommended it to the makers of physic gardens, and Dr Johnson found that a tankard of cold tea infused with a piece of the carrot-shaped root helped ease his rheumatics. Known as the all-healing plant to the ancient world and popular for its ease of cultivation, lovage is not readily found in modern nurseries. Seed is difficult to germinate, and slow to mature. It survives in shade but prefers some sun, and welcomes a chance to put down deep roots. The whole plant is intensely aromatic, somewhere between celery and fennel, but a little more peppery. Our Tudor ancestors used it as a deodorant; a few seeds dropped in the bath add a sharp, quite pleasing fragrance.

Despite another common name, love parsley, lovage has no romantic properties. The old English 'loveache' and old French *livesche* seem to come from the late Latin *levisticum*, thought to be a distortion of *ligusticum*, indicating that it was grown around Liguria in Italy. The Romans adored it. With rue, celery and bay, lovage helped spice their dishes to a degree which would seem intolerably bitter to modern palates, but probably masked other even less agreeable flavours.

*Maggikraut*, lovage's German name, opened my eyes to the fact that the famous stock-cube is named not after an Italian family called Maggi, as I had always supposed, but from its taste, resembling lovage (the seeds do make an excellent addition to a stockpot). The immensely practical Emperor Charlemagne liked lovage enough to command it to be grown in every garden; modern cooks add it to tomato salads, potato dishes, stews and salads: very little is needed. I'd also recommend trying the seeds in a soft cream cheese, or in making cheese straws. A leaf added to rhubarb brings out the taste, as do lovage stems instead of straws when drinking Bloody Marys. As a tea, it tastes quite like a vegetable soup, and makes an excellent addition to any detoxifying diet.

Culpeper recommended an infusion of lovage seeds for sore or dim eyes, and also as a gargle; fried leaves applied hot to a boil were said to bring it to bursting point. Lovage's old name of bladder seed owes little to any diuretic properties, more to confusion with its Scottish cousin *Ligusticum scoticum*, spignel or baldmoney, which like 'bladder' is a corruption of Baldur, the Apollo of northern myths.

# MARIGOLD
## *Calendula officinalis*

AN OLD GERMAN superstition declares that it's a sure sign of rain if the marigold, which shuts its petals at night, hasn't opened them again by seven in the morning. Shakespeare alludes to this in the lovely scene from *The Winter's Tale* in which Perdita, using flowers to play elegant word-games with her courtly visitors, speaks of 'The marigold, that goes to bed wi' the sun, And with him rises weeping'. In a homely evening scene in *Sons and Lovers*, D.H. Lawrence compared the first shearing of a baby's golden curls to 'the petals of a marigold scattered in the reddening firelight'.

Many people love marigolds, because they are the first flowers they grew as a child, or perhaps just because they look so cheerful. Their old or popular names in various languages verge on poetry: solis sponsa, Mary's bud, Mary Gowles, Oculus Christi, golds, ruddes, *souci des jardins* and, prettiest of all, the northern Italian *fiore d'ogni mese*. The last, like the botanical name *Calendula*, from *calendae*, the first day of the month, refers to the belief that it can be found in flower, somewhere, in every month. Slightly less picturesquely, Gerard says it is called, although only by 'the vulgar sort of women, Jacke an Apes on horseback'. He appears to be referring to the larger, double-flowered variety, hence the innuendo.

Marigold has long been used to soothe sore eyes (the distilled water of the flowers is mixed with witch hazel) and also has a reputation as a general wonder-worker for skin complaints, from nappy rash to athlete's foot. The crushed petals will soothe the pain of nettle and wasp stings, as well as mosquito bites, and the petals can be boiled and the water strained into your bath to ease aches. For an easy facial sauna, hang your head over a bowl of hot water in which you have already placed some marigold petals, or drink an infusion of them to help alleviate gastric or duodenal ulcers. Press the crushed petals against the source of a toothache. Treat painful varicose veins with the same ingredients as for an eye-bath, in the ratio of ten parts of witch hazel to one of marigold water, kept in the fridge and made up fresh each week. You can also make a home face-cleanser by stirring two tablespoons of dried petals into twice that amount of warm olive or almond oil before adding a little orange or rose water. Cooled and decanted, it will keep for at least a month in the fridge.

'Of marygold we learn that summe use [it] to make theyr here yellow with the floure of this herbe,' says one of the old herbals, tartly adding that this is only for those vain persons who are 'not beyng content with the naturall colour which God hath given them'. Be careful, however: the colour is bright and brassy, better suited to its old-fashioned use as a colorant for pale cheeses.

Marigolds are as useful in the kitchen as in the medicine cupboard. The Romans used them – and so do we – as a substitute for saffron. You can soak the petals in warm milk and use the infusion to make mildly-flavoured buns and biscuits. The petals can be added to omelettes and, according to

Gerard's *Herbal*, to soups. Such a popular culinary ingredient were marigold petals that 'in some grocers or spice-sellers' houses are to be found barrels filled with them ... insomuch that no broths are made without dried marigolds'.

At one time regarded as a symbol of endurance, the marigold was used by girls in parts of north Europe to keep tabs on absent lovers. A bit of earth was dug from the point where the lover had trodden, put in a pot and a marigold planted: if it flourished, all was well, and the lover was faithful.

A last tip, this one for the vegetable garden: try planting marigolds among potatoes to keep them disease-free. The Incas did, with great success, although the plant used was probably *Tagetes patula*, the spreading or French marigold, originating in Mexico.

# MARJORAM AND OREGANO
## *Origanum majorana, O. vulgare*

THE CONFUSION BETWEEN marjoram and oregano is partly due to the fact that *Origanum* is the species name. Pot marjoram, the white-flowered variety with which we are most familiar in the kitchen, is officially named *Origanum majorana*; the purple-flowered wild marjoram, which is more restricted in its uses, is *Origanum vulgare*.

Historically, marjoram is one of the most cheerful of herbs. *Oros* and *ganos* tell us that the Ancient Greeks warmed to it as the British do to gorse and heather, naming it 'joy of the hillside' in gratitude; sweet marjoram they also knew as *amarkos*, the Romans as *amarcus*. Marjoram brought good health and longevity, but also shared with rosemary an association with remembrance, causing it to be planted on graves and twined into wreaths for wedding feasts. Sprigs were laid in the chest of linen collected over the years in preparation for a daughter's marriage; if she wanted to know in advance who was to be her true love, she was advised to place marjoram under her pillow and expect a revealing dream.

Medicinally, the Ancient Greeks used wild marjoram to cure rheumatism, narcotic poisoning and depression. Aristotle, making careful notes on the habits of animals, observed that a tortoise will always nibble at a marjoram bush after killing a snake: if the bush is removed from reach, the tortoise dies. This, he concluded, shows that marjoram contains anti-toxic properties.

Later fans of marjoram made it into a tea which, sweetened with honey, proved an excellent throat-soother. But in the days when keeping her home smelling agreeable was a housewife's daily nightmare, marjoram's chief attraction was its sweet but aromatic smell. Bunches of the leaves were squeezed to produce an oil for rubbing over wooden furniture, placed in muslin bags to scent clothes and linen, and scattered among the rushes on the floor.

Marjoram's significance as a herb of joy made it popular with poets. Shakespeare has the Clown in *All's Well that Ends Well* refer to a woman as 'the sweet marjoram of the salad'; while Perdita, in *The Winter's Tale*, tempts an admiring visitor with the prospect of inhaling 'hot lavender, mints, savory, marjoram', a heady enough combination of smells to put any suitor in her power. In Sonnet 99 Shakespeare conventionally accuses the lily of stealing its fairness from his beloved's hand, and the violet her sweet breath – and then, odder by far, asserted that 'buds of marjoram had stol'n thy hair'.

John Dryden, introducing his great translation of the *Aeneid*, was anxious that his patron Lord Normandy – and his readers – should appreciate the subtleties he had worked so hard to convey. Virgil referred to Venus depositing Cupid on a bed of *mollis amaracus* and the innuendo had not escaped Dryden – *'mollis amaracus'* also conveys the sense of sweet lovemaking – but 'If I should translate it sweet marjoram, as the word signifies, the reader would think I had mistaken Virgil.' That would be dreadful: and clever Dryden, · while appearing anxious, in fact alerts the reader to the excellence of his translation.

Mrs Grieve tells us that a dull purple dye for wool used to be produced from the flowering tops of wild marjoram, and also mentions its use in dairies. A sprig of marjoram placed beside the churn helped prevent the milk from turning sour in a storm.

Marjoram's use in cooking depends on the sort you have picked. Sweet marjoram is delicious in a salad dressing, wild marjoram is better with meat-based sauces and pasta dishes. Real enthusiasts should consider growing several different kinds, for it is easier to judge what is wanted by the smell and taste of a leaf than to worry about precisely which form or species the leaf comes from.

After all, marjoram is a member of the same family as the proliferating mints, and there are about fifty different species, forms and cultivars: why complicate life when your nose and tongue can do the work so easily?

# MEADOWSWEET
## *Filipendula ulmaria*

TEMPTED FOR A moment by Menelaus's invitation in the *Odyssey* to stay on and enjoy the comforts of his mainland home, Odysseus's son Telemachus wistfully compares it to his own home on the dry, infertile island of Ithaca. There, he says sadly, no plain is verdant enough to produce the rolling fields of oats, barley and meadowsweet over which Helen's former husband presides; nevertheless, the call of family duty is strong and Telemachus takes his leave.

Meadowsweet has a mass of pretty names, including bridewort and queen of the meadow, but it is the Latin name Linnaeus gave it, *Spiraea ulmaria*, which should interest us most. *Ulmaria* merely indicates the similarity of its leaves to those of elm, *Ulmus*, but *spiraea* provided the main element of the word 'aspirin', the name the grateful firm of Bayer devised for the wonder compound they registered in 1899. We think of aspirin in connection with the bark of the white willow (*Salix alba*), recommended by Hippocrates in 400 BC to ease pain and fever. Salicin, an extract of willow bark, was first obtained in 1828, leading to the discovery of ways to manufacture a synthetic form of salicylic acid. But this was far from satisfactory.

The breakthrough came at the Bayer dyeworks when two chemists produced acetylated spiralic acid – from which aspirin took its name – from the flowers of meadowsweet. (Two weeks later, in September 1897, the two men, Felix Hoffman and Arthur Eichengrun, acetylated morphine, and produced heroin).

While aspirin can cause gastric ulcers when taken in large amounts, meadowsweet, taken as a tea made from the flower-heads, shares the anti-inflammatory effect of aspirin while protecting the lining of the stomach and intestines. For this reason it was frequently recommended in Victorian herbals as a safe treatment for children with diarrhoea, and as an all-round easer of any form of stomach upset.

Meadowsweet was one of the three sacred herbs of the Druids – the others were water-mint and vervain – whose use for it has not been recorded. A party of intoxicated pagan priests is a pleasant thought, however, and the almond-scented flowers were a popular ingredient of herbal beers long before medieval times. It is probable that the country name derives from the use of the flower in making mead, rather than from the decorative presence and scent of those broad white flowerheads in summer meadows.

In Elizabethan times, the delicate fragrance of meadowsweet made it one of the most popular of the strewing-herbs with which floors were scattered in the summer months. Queen Elizabeth would have nothing but meadowsweet mingled with the rushes on her bedroom floor, and no wonder: 'the smell thereof makes the heart merrie and joyful and delighteth the senses,' wrote John Gerard.

Another way of making the heart merry, according to Gerard, was to boil meadowsweet flowers in wine; Culpeper also recommended adding a leaf of it to claret to bestow 'a fine relish'. Less reliable is his suggestion for raising blisters by applying the full-grown leaves to the skin. You might prefer to try Mrs Grieve's suggestion of an infusion of the dried flowers – they should be picked in July – with honey and boiling water as a treatment for fever. While nowhere near so effective as an infusion of feverfew leaves, meadowsweet flowers are also a good treatment for headaches.

A further use for meadowsweet, for anybody anxious to add an original touch to their wedding-night preparations, is to arrange for the bedroom floor to be covered with the herbs of Venus (erotic love) and Mars (combat). For Venus, use meadow-sweet, verbena, marjoram, mint, thyme, valerian and violet; for Mars, scatter basil and broom flowers.

# MILK THISTLE
## *Silybum marianum*

Hans Christian Anderson told a story about the purple thistle which, plucked by a Scots gentleman to carry into a castle for a buttonhole, dreams of having his whole family upgraded to a life of baronial style. He expects, at the very least, to be awarded a medal of honour. No such luck for the poor thistle – but Anderson neatly rounds the story off by pointing out that he did, at least, get written about.

One tradition connects *Silybum marianum*, the milk or Marian thistle, with Mary Queen of Scots, who is supposed to have planted it on Dumbarton Rock. It would seem more appropriate for her to have planted the spear thistle, *Cirsium vulgare*, which is carried (with caution, being fiendishly thorny) in various ancient ceremonies designed to warn Scottish lairds not to push their tenants too hard on the matter of property rights.

A more ancient tradition connects this singular thistle, often grown in gardens for its handsome looks, to the Virgin Mary, whose milk is said to have fallen on the plant, thus causing the white veins on the leaves which single it out from all other species. If you are interested in making a Marian garden, based on the enclosed plot of medieval times, the tall purple-flowered thistles might be planted at the back instead of the more conventional larkspur (Mary's tears). Until I began to research herbs, it hadn't struck me quite how many qualify for a place in a Mary garden. Just for a start, there is alchemilla (Lady's mantle), forget-me-not (Mary's eyes), and mullein (Lady's candle). If you want to imagine dressing her, you should put a bluebell (Lady's thimble) on her finger, a cowslip (Our Lady's keys) at her waist, and a flourishing plot of scabious nearby for her well-stocked pincushion. Mary Garden enthusiasts will already know the significance of irises, roses and lilies, especially the lofty Madonna lily, featured in so many renaissance interpretations of the Annunciation.

Back to our prickly friend. All thistles used to be valued as a food source. The Romans boiled the roots; one seventeenth-century cookery book declares that 'the young shoots, in the spring, cut close to the root with part of the stalk on, is one of the best boiling sallets that can be eaten, and surpasses the finest cabbage.' As a cure for wounds, another author suggests that an infusion of 'blessed thistle' should be drunk for nine consecutive mornings, and again after a nine-day space, followed by a diet of cows' milk and wheat bread. Precisely how is unclear, but various medieval writers recommend milk thistle for its protective powers against the plague.

The connection between the milk thistle and breast-feeding has a long history, and most modern herbalists would still recommend a thrice-daily tisane of it to nursing mothers for safety and good results. The surprise, as so often with herbs, lies in finding that the latest trend is only an old custom rediscovered. Milk thistle's modern reputation as a beat-the-hangover cure started about ten years ago, but a Mr Westmacott was saying much the same thing back in 1694. The Marian thistle, he wrote, 'is a friend to the Liver and Blood ... but as the World decays, so doth the use of good old things, and others more delicate and less virtuous [are] brought in.'

Milk thistle's reputation as a cure for gall-bladder-related conditions was established long before Mr Westmacott's time and today it is among the herbal bestsellers, beloved of anybody whose work requires heavy-duty socialising and drinking. Why is it so effective? *The Encyclopaedia of Natural Medicine* informs us that 'the common milk thistle contains some of the most potent liver protective substances known, a mixture of three flavanoligans collectively referred to as silymarin.' The main chemical component, silybin, defends the body against the detrimental effects of drugs, drink, environmental toxins and chemotherapy; silybin is often used to treat liver disease. Given in injected form, it also offers a necessarily speedy antidote to poisoning by the death-cap mushroom. (Now, if only the Empress Livia's family had been told that, think what a difference it would have made to Rome's imperial history.)

# MINT
*Mentha piperita, M. viridis*

To drink my first cup of mint tea by the side of an open drain in Tangiers was not the best introduction to it, but by the end of that holiday I was haggling with carpet-sellers simply for the pleasure of being served tall glasses of the hot, sweet, amber-coloured liquid. Teabags are fine, but only until you've tried making mint tea straight from the plant: there is no comparison.

Offered as a simple form of hospitality, peppermint tea is an instant cooler. Tiny glands on the leaves contain menthol which, released by heat, induces perspiration. Infused in hot milk, peppermint eases stomach pains, while a tisane of peppermint and elderflower has long been considered an excellent remedy in the early stages of colds or 'flu. It is not clear why the Greeks and Romans liked to crown themselves with peppermint, but they knew the digestive benefits of following a large meal with mint tea (our habit of eating after-dinner mints dates all the way back to those ancient banquets). Menthe, in Greek mythology, was a pretty nymph turned into a humble creeping plant by Persephone when she noticed Pluto's interest in her. Pluto consoled the nymph by ensuring that she would smell delicious however hard she was trodden down.

As well as benefiting the digestion peppermint, tested against paracetamol, has performed well as a cure for headaches. There is some evidence to suggest that it stimulates the memory, and it also has a good reputation for calming the nerves. The leaves, rubbed on itches or burns, soothe them as the menthol is released onto the skin. Steamed and placed over closed eyes, peppermint leaves are an instant refresher.

Peppermint first appears in the English herbals in a book written by the botanist John Ray in 1696, and was listed in the *London Pharmacopoeia* of 1721. Mitcham in Surrey specialised in growing peppermint, and by 1850, 500 acres were devoted to it – a large area was needed for crop rotation, since true *Mentha piperita*, if it is being grown for commercial use, can only be cultivated in the same spot for two consecutive years. The oil produced from English plants is regarded by experts as the best; America produces much more, chiefly for the chewing-gum market, but it is of relatively poor quality.

God forbid that you should be harassed by rats, but if you are, a judicious scattering of rags soaked in peppermint oil will keep them out of your way: they hate the smell, as do ants and fleas. I know someone who rubs her dog with mint leaves for this reason. Butterflies and bees will thank you for keeping mint in the garden – but a word of warning: the roots should be confined, as otherwise they will spread like tentacles.

The culinary history of mint is venerable. Baucis and Philemon scrubbed the table with mint leaves before setting it with food suitable for the gods; the Romans thought the smell of spearmint stimulated the appetite and used it to flavour sauces and jellies, much as we eat it today with roast lamb. A newer tip is to add a little chopped mint to omelettes or scrambled eggs, just in the final cooking stage. It does wonders for salads, if sparingly used, and for peas. Dieters might like to ruminate on the fact that peppermint is famous for assisting in the digestion of fatty foods, while smokers tired of chewing parsley could turn to mint instead: no herb has a more impressive reputation for conquering the smell of tobacco.

Poets have not been inspired by peppermint, but Dickens drew on his own memories to describe young David Copperfield being employed by his schoolmate Steerforth to tell him stories every evening in exchange for help with his sums. When David's voice grew hoarse, he was restored with a drop of cowslip wine in which Steerforth had thoughtfully diluted a peppermint drop. The peppermint-flavoured cordial quaffed by the matron and Mr Beadle in *Oliver Twist* is more likely to have been gin with peppermint added, again to disguise the fact.

# MULLEIN
## *Verbascum thapsus*

IT'S HARD TO think of another plant with so many
and such strange popular names as the tall and
beautiful mullein. Mrs Grieve lists thirty-one, of
which the following are some of the most striking:
Adam's flannel, shepherd's staff, velvet plant,
Cuddy's lungs, beggar's blanket, rag paper, candlewick plant, hag's taper, hare's beard, duffle and clot.

The mullein is not an endangered species. Its
proud spikes of brilliant yellow flowers rising from
furry rosettes of leaves flourish from the Himalayas
to Ireland, wherever a piece of chalky wasteland is
to be found. It is a plant unusually good at taking
care of itself: those hairy grey leaves and stalks,
anathema to hungry animals or creeping insects,
also help to reduce evaporation in dry conditions.

'Candlewick plant' gives a clue to one early use,
as a wick for lamps. Dipped in tallow, the stalks
were used as torches: children still carry them in the
Greek Good Friday processions, when candles are
ceremonially borne from village to village. Renaissance ladies used the bright yellow flowers, rubbing
them into wet hair before combing it up through
flat-brimmed crownless hats to dry in the sun, to
encourage fashionable blondness. Poacher-fishermen
sprinkled the narcotic seeds on water to stupefy their

prey. Shepherds and wanderers gathered the furry leaves to put in their shoes as thermal protection, and anyone caught short by a mullein-decked roadside will gratefully use them as nature's best lavatory paper.

Gerard gathered his mullein supplies on Highgate Hill in the days when lilies grew wild on Hampstead Heath and mallow thrived below the gallows at Tyburn. Mullein, he wrote, was a wonderful remedy for cattle with infected lungs; until the beginning of the twentieth century it was still cultivated in Irish gardens as a cure for consumption. But mullein also had a reputation for magical properties: Ulysses used it to guard against Circe's wiles and Gerard noted that a young mullein stalk, carried in the pocket, offered protection against the falling sickness, especially if gathered when the sun was in Virgo and the moon in Aries. But he was sceptical: this is most 'vaine and superstitious', he added.

Piles, warts, coughs, haemorrhoids, earache, toothache, diarrhoea: there is almost nothing for which mullein has not been recommended. When making a medicinal tisane, use a fine strainer, for the tiny hairs that cover the plant find their way through almost anything, and tickle mercilessly. Earache can be treated by two drops of juice squeezed from the leaves onto a plug of cotton-wool.

Easy to grow and ugly only when its leaves wither to tobacco-brown rags, the mullein does have one major disadvantage as a garden plant: as nectar to the bee, so is mullein to the slug...

# PARSLEY
*Petroselinum crispum*

O GDEN NASH, DESPERATE for a rhyme, chained
'parsley' to 'garsley' and did one of our most
agreeable herbs a cruel injustice. I can't, seeing
parsley sprouting plumply to form a perfect border
for the vegetable patch, feel anything less than love
for it. Parsley is easy to grow, good to taste and, a
tiny and unruly hedge alongside the ranks of
carrots, a glory to behold. It's also, as we all know,
the best cure for smelly breath ever to have been
discovered. 'Garsley'? How could he!

Parsley apparently first sprang up where the
blood of Archemorus stained the ground when he
was devoured by a serpent and, as the harbinger of
death, was dedicated to Persephone, the unhappy
queen of the Underworld. The Greeks used parsley
to decorate their tombs and to crown their athletes;
they also fed it to their horses to give them energy
for long campaigns. Roman diners donned wreaths
of parsley in the hope of staying sober, and placed
it on dishes of food to protect them from contami-
nation: neither can have been of much help.

Rich in Vitamin C and calcium, parsley found
favour in medieval times for its warming effects
and benefit to the digestion. Hildegard of Bingen
dosed her patients with parsley wine; you can make

your own by boiling ten large parsley sprigs with a quart of wine (either colour will do) for ten minutes. Stir in 9 ounces of honey and then strain into bottles. A tablespoonful three times a day is suggested.

The botanical name *Petroselinum* comes from *petros*, the Greek word for stone or rock, so it is no surprise that parsley has a long history as a cure for problems connected with kidney stones. *Petroselinum* became, in due course, petersylinge, persele and, eventually, parsley. Old herbals urge you to serve it with boiled onions as a cure for gravel, stone, or dropsy; Turner followed Pliny in suggesting that sick fish could be helped to recover by a scattering of parsley on their pond. Another adviser suggests that a woman friend should hand parsley to any young lady wanting to become pregnant. 'Sow parsley on a Good Friday', warns one well-wisher, while another offers the terrifying information that you will die within the year if you buy a house which has no parsley nearby.

Lay parsley leaves on sore eyes to cool them, if you are happy to take Nicholas Culpeper's suggestion, and smear fried parsley over aching breasts. You could eat it to stop yourself getting rheumatism – but be warned: this tip comes from a herbalist who thinks you can keep yourself in fantastic condition by carrying a potato in your pocket.

Yet it's never wise to mock. The *British Herbal Compendium* (1992) also commends parsley for rheumatism, while its reputation for curing kidney infections was proved in the First World War, when parsley tea was found to be one of the best and most readily available cures for dysentery sufferers in the trenches.

Mrs Grieve discovered in the 1930s that the French were using a pounded mixture of parsley and snails to bring down swellings and treat potentially cancerous tumours. The application of the crushed leaves, she added, seemed to soothe bites and stings. They are also commended as a cure for foot-rot in sheep and as a beneficial addition to a dog's diet. I scoffed at this last, having seen our own spaniel reject everything green, from marrows to *mangetout*. Surprisingly, however, a handful of chopped parsley added to her dinner-bowl proved perfectly acceptable. This quantity every three days or so is suggested.

*Gremolada*, an Italian sauce eaten with *osso bucco*, also goes well with any braised meat. You make it by sautéing chopped parsley with minced garlic, lemon zest and a squeeze of lemon; spread over the meat just before serving.

# ROSEMARY
## *Rosmarinus officinalis*

ONE POPULAR NAME for rosemary, sea-dew, comes from the light, luminous colour of the flowers which, from a distance, can look as blue as a patch of sunlit morning sea (though not, of course, if it is that pretty variety 'Majorca Pink'). Happiest in chalky soil, it will also thrive for thirty years or more in a large pot: don't worry about the old adage that only a forceful wife makes rosemary flourish, one which apparently so agitated the hearts of Elizabethan gentlemen that they would break off the heads of too-thriving rosemary bushes. Rosemary will, of course, prosper for either sex, so long as you remember to prune it after flowering and don't blame yourself for the fact that it hates wet English winters. A cheerful green appearance should never stop you taking a few cuttings as a precaution; rosemary bushes have a cruel way of rotting slowly from the roots up, yielding their dark secret only when it's too late for remedies. They will flourish best planted near a south-facing brick wall which retains and reflects whatever heat is available.

Rosemary, like mint, is said to be of great benefit to a crop of cabbages; it is good for town-dwellers too, giving them something more agreeable to sniff at than exhaust fumes when walking along a busy road, so plant it to face the street and you'll do everyone a favour. One of the most attractive varieties is the rambling 'Severn Sea', which does well in containers, but my own favourite is 'Miss Jessopp's Upright' which, as its name suggests, is tall, thin and energetic.

The Ancient Greeks discovered that rosemary benefits the circulation. Students bound wreaths of it to their brows to help their memories, a property for which it was still being praised in Elizabethan times. We have a Frenchwoman to thank for introducing it to England, the Countess of Hainault, mother-in-law of Edward III. Sir Thomas More loved it, not only for the sake of his bees, but 'because it is the herb sacred to remembrance, and therefore, to friendship'. The medieval herbalists had been equally enthusiastic. Rosemary was recommended as a hair rinse, as a wash for the skin 'to wax shiny', and as a tooth powder, made from the ashes of rosemary twigs. Mixed with colt's-foot, it was smoked as a cure for coughs; placed in drawers, it scented linen; laid under beds, it helped keep troubling dreams away.

Christmas revellers used to decorate their halls with rosemary and bay as well as holly and ivy, according to Herrick. Italians and Spaniards grew rosemary to ward off witches; the fourteenth-century Queen Isabella of Hungary dabbed her ancient and paralysed limbs with rosemary distilled in alcohol, recovered her agility, and grew so youthful that the amorous King of Poland proposed to her (hence Hungary Water, popular throughout the eighteenth century and still sometimes sold by beauty-conscious pharmacies). Don Quixote had his wounded ear dressed with a poultice of chewed rosemary leaves and salt; Edgar, in *King Lear*, seems to have been alluding to an actual practice when he described

'Bedlam beggars' – madmen – scarifying their limbs with rosemary twigs.

Modern uses of rosemary include the manufacture of eau-de-Cologne, of which it is a prime ingredient. You can munch a leaf or two as a breath-freshener, or infuse them as a tension-easing tea. Boil a handful and strain to make a hair-rinse. The pure oil is most beneficial here, however: rub in a few drops after towel-drying, and you can expect shiny, wonderfully fragrant hair. Go easy with rosemary body oil: it is very powerful as a stimulant.

Famously delicious with roast lamb, rosemary tastes better still if anchovies are used too: into each stab in the lamb flesh push a sprig of rosemary, a small piece of peeled garlic and about half a tinned anchovy. Mix what is left in the tin with a large knob of butter and spread on top. Put in a roasting tin with half a bottle of dry white wine and cook as preferred. Use the juice for gravy.

# RUE
## *Ruta graveolens*

Rue's botanical name gives away its best and its worst sides. Some derive *ruta* from the Greek *reuo*, to set free, honouring the plant as a liberator from both illness and witches' spells. *Graveolens* means heavily-scented, and the smell of rue is not delicious, but the yellowy-green glaucous leaves will grace any garden and look particularly good planted with rosemary and feathery grey-green santolina. Grown in moist and well-drained soil, the leaves will assume a more bluish green, especially in the variety 'Jackman's Blue' – my mother's favourite – which thrives in shade.

There is a practical reason for confining rue to dark corners: the leaves react with sunlight, causing burns which can be surprisingly severe. So be sure to wear gloves if you're planning to clip your rue on a sunny day in April – the best month for pruning it.

Edgar Allen Poe is one of the few writers to have been excited by the acrid smell of this herb. In 'For Annie', a morbid ditty written in 1849, a dying man hallucinates about 'beautiful Puritan pansies' and the scent of rue before Annie (death) wraps him in her night-black hair. Aristotle, who knew rue was the only plant a basilisk or cockatrice could not wither with one glance, took note of the fact that a weasel will always feed on wild rue before taking on a snake (reason: the snake hates the smell).

'There's rue for you; and here's some for me; we may call it herb of grace o' Sundays,' says Ophelia, with less madness than we might think. 'Herb of grace' was the name given to rue in medieval times when it was tied into sprigs for dipping and sprinkling holy water in churches before mass. French churchgoers carried bunches of it on Palm Sunday, to be dipped in a tub of holy water and carried home, where the sharp smell would remind them of the need for contrition. Judges and court officials of the time carried it for another purpose, to protect themselves from the notorious gaol fever spread by fleas and cockroaches in filthy prisons. (Rue is a powerful insecticide: medieval housewives sprinkled their floors with rue water to keep down fleas.)

Rue's medicinal value has been established since ancient times. Mithridates recommended it as an antidote to poison, and it was given to Ulysses to protect him against the spells of the island witch, Circe. Artists knew rue as a marvellous eye-strengthener and its effects, when used as a weak daily eye-wash, were well known to painters of the renaissance period. Sceptics should note that rutin, found in rue, has been used for its strengthening effect on the capillaries for the last fifty years.

The Romans who brought rue to England used it both as a palliative for sore eyes and as a digestive. For more superstitious reasons epileptics in the Middle Ages were given garlands of rue to hang around their necks. It was a period which saw rue both as a defence against witches and as a sure way to gain second sight (it is not clear whether there was any connection between this notion and rue's known benefit to the eyes). Medieval herbalists also recommended chewing rue leaves to cure dizzy spells, and modern authors agree with them: a weak rue tisane is still suggested as a treatment for headaches and flatulence, and for menstrual cramps. As to the flavour, it's on a par with St John's Wort tea. I wouldn't drink it twice. Pregnant women shouldn't drink it at all.

The bitter taste comes from the rutin, also found in orange peel and capers; *grappa con ruta* is an Italian aperitif to which a sprig of the herb has been added. Putting just a leaf in an egg or cheese dish or in tomato sauce gives it extra zip; if the thought makes you wince, blanch the leaf in boiling water first to reduce the bitterness.

Unconnected with the French word for street, rue becomes more comical in other languages: *rude* in Danish, *ruda* in Spanish and *sudah* in Urdu. But the Chinese have the best of it: *chow-cho* may not be the most useful word to know, but has a charm *Ruta graveolens* somehow lacks.

# SAGE
## *Salvia officinalis*

'AND SAGE, THEY drank, to keep their limbs from haemorrhage,' Chaucer's knight recalled, drawing attention to its reputation as the medieval gentleman's cure for all ailments. Sage produced quite different thoughts in Walt Whitman's mind as he described the amorous pollen-gathering of 'the hairy wild bee that ... grips the full-grown lady-flower, curves upon her with amorous firm legs, takes his will of her' on a bed scented by apples, birch-bark and sage.

Beginning as *salvia*, from the Latin *salvere*, to save (or *servire*, to serve), the name was corrupted to *sawge* and thus to sage. The tribute implied in the derivation is only a slight exaggeration, for the properties of sage are indeed remarkable. Research is currently being undertaken to see if it can be used to defeat Alzheimer's disease, a fact which brings us intriguingly close to our forebears, since the Ancient Greeks and Romans valued sage above all as a mental stimulant. The Chinese, in the early years of trading with Britain, were prepared to exchange four pounds of their tea for a pound of sage leaves, which gives a clear indication of the medicinal value they placed on the latter. For teeth and gums, fresh leaves are best: sage's reputation as a cure for gingivitis is well-established, and rubbing the velvety leaves over teeth will clean them while freshening the breath. They taste better than toothpaste.

Sage has a staggeringly wide variety of uses. A handful of the cat's-tongue-shaped leaves mixed with lavender, rosemary and thyme makes a household cleanser. Leave them for three weeks in as sunny a spot as you can find, in an unstoppered jar filled up with white vinegar. Strain the liquid before use. If you fancy making a sage aftershave, infuse sage and rosemary with cider vinegar for a week, strain and add an equal quantity of witch hazel. Greying hair? Boil dried sage leaves with teapot leftovers for half an hour, strain, and then massage into towel-dried hair four times a week to produce a fairly convincing dark colour while helping the hair grow, and look glossy. But no more delicious meals of *fegato al salvia* for would-be parents: an Arabian herbal tells us that the mixture of sage and wine, as in this delicious way of cooking liver, is a splendid contraceptive. Please don't rely on it.

Medieval gardeners took care always to grow sage: 'He that would live for aye, Must eat sage in May,' they chanted, parroting their Roman predecessors who knew that the man *cui salvia crescit in horto* was taking care of himself. In ancient times sage was treated with such respect that offerings of bread and wine were made to the ground where it grew. Known to produce the only brew for serious thinkers, it was also praised for its ability to reduce night sweats, and – this was of great importance in the days when spices were a rare commodity – as a preservative for meat.

Sage as an essential ingredient of stuffing, especially for pork and turkey, needs no recommendation; sage cheese has been made since at least the seventeenth century and is, if you rate the herb's benefit to your digestion, memory, skin and emotional state, tastier than a sage tisane. To make sage tea, infuse an ounce of dried leaves with an ounce of sugar, the juice of a lemon and a pinch of grated lemon rind in a quart of boiling water, and strain after half an hour. If you enjoy re-creating historical experiences, this is what American patriots disguised as Mohawk Indians were obliged to drink after they had tipped all 342 of the East India Company's tax-bearing tea-chests into Boston Harbor in 1773.

The charming tradition of planting sage-bushes on graves noted by Samuel Pepys has not survived; it may have stemmed from the herb's reputation for alleviating sadness.

# SOAPWORT
*Saponaria officinalis*

THE BOTANICAL NAME, *Saponaria officinalis*, is a giveaway, *sapo* being the Latin for soap. Soapwort provided an efficient early cleaner for both skin and materials: rub its pointed leaves between your fingers, and the froth begins to form which gave it the name 'foamweed'. National Trust conservators use a soapwort preparation developed by the owner of Uppark for cleaning precious textiles. I can vouch for it myself, after seeing the 'before' and 'after' state of some Jacobean hangings once so filthy that the deep blue crewel stitching looked like a sea of tar.

'Bouncing Bet' is the name the Elizabethans gave soapwort. Did the bulbous calyx and scalloped petals of the flower suggest a jolly laundress displaying her rear in a froth of pink petticoats as she scrubbed away? Hedge pink, old maid's pink, crow soap, sheepweed and bruisewort are some of its less familiar nicknames. 'Bruisewort' acknowledges the soothing effect of a decoction made from the root, or a poultice of fresh leaves.

River banks are often thick with soapwort in the summer, but anglers dislike it near fish ponds, and gardeners tend to steer clear of a herb which has ruthless colonising tendencies. But soapwort used to be popular for the 'decking of houses', and 'hedge pink' is a reminder that it once grew as thickly as grass by the roadside. It was called 'London Pride', because of the many bunches sold at Covent Garden in Georgian times for the sake of its aromatic scent, a spicy mixture of raspberries and cloves.

Argument continues about whether soapwort was the *struthium* praised by Pliny for its cleansing abilities, even though *struthium* was said to be tall and prickly, and soapwort is prickle-free and seldom taller than a foot and a half. Its reputation as a cleansing agent certainly dates back thousands of years, for Biblical references to the use of soap clearly allude to herbal sources, and soapwort was widely grown in the ancient world. In medieval England it was known as 'the fuller's plant', from its use in the process of cleaning and thickening cloth, and shepherds in parts of the Swiss Alps still use it as a sheep dip before shearing, a practice that can be traced back to the first century AD. Textile magnates of the nineteenth century cultivated fields of soapwort for just this purpose, both in Britain and America.

There are many tributes to the value of the roots and leaves of soapwort as a treatment for skin diseases, including severe acne, boils and abscesses. Gerard tells us the ladies of his time used soapwort in the bath to beautify themselves; it probably works better, if it works at all, taken as a tisane – but with caution, because of its saponin content.

# SOLOMON'S SEAL
## *Polygonatum multiflorum*

RICHARD MABEY, IN his *Flora Brittanica*, describes the pleasure of coming across Solomon's seal in a spring wood, the delicate scrolls of its green leaves unfurling just before the blossoming of the row of scented, hanging, bell-like flowers. It is related to the delicate lily-of-the-valley, but the udderlike droop of the row of flowers earned it the less romantic Dorsetshire name – now defunct – of sow's tits.

Solomon's seal is a more baffling name, perhaps originating from the fact that the thick rootstock, when cut transversely, reveals markings which have been thought to resemble a group of Hebrew letters. Readers of the *Arabian Nights* will remember that Solomon's seal was a prestigious symbol of authority, and most of the early herbalists believed the name to be an affirmation of the plant's effectiveness as a healer of cuts. Lists of Marian flowers include Solomon's seal as the property of the Virgin, *Sigillum Sanctae Mariae*. The botanical name, *Polygonatum multiflorum*, is more easily unravelled. *Multiflorum* is self-explanatory and *polys* is the Greek for 'many'. 'Gonatum' comes either from *gony*, knee-joint, referring to the many small knee-like nodes on the stems, or from *gonos*, offspring, in allusion to the numerous seeds.

Pretty though the plant looks, beware of eating any part of it, especially the berries: only the roots, lifted in autumn, are of medicinal value. Creeping and white, they spread themselves with ease, throwing up tall sappy stems with large, oval, ribbed leaves.

Convallarin, also found in lily-of-the-valley, is the magic ingredient in Solomon's seal. 'That which might be written of this herb as touching the knitting of bones, and that truly, would seem unto some incredible,' John Gerard gushed in his *Herbal*, and went on to say that there was 'not to be found another herb comparable to it for the purposes aforesaid'. The method he gave (used, according to his account, by 'the vulgar sort of people of Hampshire') required the roots to be crushed and then mixed with ale as a drink which would guarantee a rapid healing of fractures and easing of bruises. On the subject of how such bruises might have come about, he was unexpectedly coy. They might have been caused by falls, 'or women's wilfulness in stumbling upon their hastie husband's fists, or such like.' Was Gerard putting in a quiet word for abused wives? On the subject of physical attacks, another medieval recipe recommends applying the crushed roots to black eyes (there's nothing like a herbal for pointing up the violence of medieval times – just try counting the number of cures given for wounds, broken bones and bruises).

John Parkinson was among those who extolled the value of Solomon's seal as a poultice for bruises, and as the sole ingredient of a distilled water – it was made from the whole plant – which lightened the skin and took away wrinkles and the effects of sunburn. Culpeper commented on the popularity of this distillation among Italian women, and noted that it was sold by most fashionable perfumers (its high price, he shrewdly noted, was unrelated to any difficulty in obtaining the ingredients). Enthusiasts should note that lupins, made into a paste with lemon juice and the gall of a goat, were thought to be even more effective as a complexion-improver.

Mrs Grieve noted that the flowers and roots have been used both as a form of snuff and as an aphrodisiac. Solomon's seal also has value as a cure for piles, four ounces of the roots being simmered with a pint of molasses and two pints of water. A white witch tells me that the roots can also be burned in order to seal a spell.

# ST JOHN'S WORT
## *Hypericum perforatum*

SHORT ON NICKNAMES, St John's wort is unusually strong in the magic department: *hypereikon*, its name in Classical Greek, means 'power over an apparition', while *perforatum* refers to the minute 'perforations' in the leaves, actually resin glands, which give off the sharp smell once supposed to keep witches at bay. A sprig placed under your pillow will give you the comforting protection of John the Baptist against evil spirits. To make absolutely sure of keeping them away, flourish the sprig in front of you while saying: 'Trefoil, vervain, St John's wort, dill, Hinder witches of their will.'

Midsummer is held to be a particularly potent time for herbs. The feast of St John, 24th June, when bonfires in honour of the saint were kindled in parts of Germany and Austria was conveniently celebrated on Walpurgisnacht, when ancient rural communities brought good luck to their crops with fire-rituals. Engaged couples jumped over the fire to establish by the height of their leap how long their days of married bliss would last. In Brittany, any girl prepared to dance around nine of these fires could be sure of finding a husband before the year was out – if nothing else, her energy must have guaranteed the interest of a few suitors. A French proverb tells of using 'all the herbs of St John' to bring about a love-affair. The user was expected to fast for twenty-four hours and then go out before sunrise on St John's Day to pick the herbs – which, if these conditions were met, would never wither. A childless woman could make herself fertile by the simple act of walking through her vegetable garden, unclothed, on St John's Eve.

Nobody could object to the bright golden flowers of hypericum, but it is not the plant's good looks which have made it one of the world's popular herbs. It was recognised as an impressive healer of wounds even in the days of Hippocrates, and the English long had great faith in its ability to protect their homes from a lightning strike. More recently it has become celebrated as an effective remedy for mild depression. As someone once resigned to waking daily in a state of inexplicable gloom, I can promise you it works, but you must allow at least a month for the miraculous effects to begin. It is reputedly also effective as a sedative, and even as a hangover cure. But don't eat the plant itself: all you'll get is tummy-ache, and red fingers from the sap.

I've had no luck tracking down the receipt for the mysterious Ointment of Elemi, involving St John's wort and turpentine, invented by a sixteenth-century Spanish doctor working in Amsterdam. As a consolation, here is an easily prepared ointment to soothe scalds, sunburn and grazes. Pack a glass jar with the flowers, pour oil over them (cold-pressed walnut or sunflower is best), seal the jar and stand it in a sunny place for a couple of weeks. Strain through a jelly bag into a jar or bottle of dark glass and keep in a cool place. St John's wort is widely available in capsule form. Sometimes referred to as the 'joy pill', it won't make you radiant: what it will do is help vanquish any groundless sense of despair or sadness.

# TANSY
*Tanacetum vulgare*

D.H. LAWRENCE BROUGHT this handsome herb into literature with his description in *Sons and Lovers* of the Morels' tansy-bordered garden path leading down to a view across red-roofed cottages to a hillside basking in autumn sunshine. Tansy was a favourite domestic remedy in Lawrence's time; nowadays, because it must be taken in carefully regulated doses, herbalists no longer recommend it.

Visually tansy is charming, tall and sturdy, with finely divided fernlike leaves and the flat yellow flowers which have given it the name 'buttons'. Kept under control, it makes a good border plant or path edging, but its colonising impulse is strong and it will take over the garden if given the chance. On the plus side, it will thrive pretty well anywhere.

As an insecticide, there's nothing to beat tansy: no wasp, butterfly or aphid will venture near its camphor scent. Scatter the (dried) leaves over kitchen shelves to keep away ants; rub them over a dog's coat, and enough tanacetin oil will be released to keep fleas away. An old book of household tips suggests scattering tansy leaves near animal bedding.

Like medieval folk, a few old-fashioned farmworkers today put sprigs of tansy in their shoes to keep aches and pains away; I've even read of it as an antidote to malaria. It was also used against the plague, and was surprisingly effective: the rats that carried the fleas that spread the plague loathed the smell, and gave it a wide berth.

Once used in large doses to procure abortions, tansy was nevertheless recommended by Nicholas Culpeper as a fertility drug. 'Let those women that desire children love this herb,' he wrote; 'it is their best companion, husbands excepted.' Later herbalists recommended infusions of tansy flowers and leaves against hysteria, and for warming yourself up on a cold day. Robert Thornton, writing in 1810, was impressed by its value as a cure for gout, recounting the story of a man who suffered from it for fifteen years and cured himself with a nightly cup of cold tansy tea. Thornton also knew of tansy's use as a digestive herb, while its reputation for expelling worms dates back to the time when intestinal ailments often followed the Lenten diet of not always fresh fish.

Tansy's botanical name *Tanacetum* is thought to derive from *athanasia*, the Greek word for immortality, perhaps a tribute to its long-lived flowers, or its use in funeral rites as a means of preserving the body from corruption. Zeus, arriving on earth disguised as an eagle, gave tansy to Ganymede, most gorgeous of mortals, to guarantee his eternal life as cupbearer to the gods. Or so the story goes.

The herb was dedicated to the Virgin Mary, a connection not easily explained, and traditionally consumed in the post-Lenten months in cakes or puddings known as 'tansies'. It's possible that tansy symbolised the bitter herbs eaten at the Jewish Passover feast, which coincides with Easter, but Christian writers often connect it with the ending of the Lenten fast, as a digestive or blood purifier.

Tansy cakes were used in a ball-game played at Easter between clergymen and their parishioners; the victor was given a larger tansy cake as his prize.

Tansy tea is an acquired taste, and I'd prefer to recommend peppermint or camomile for a tummy upset. Remember that this exceptionally powerful herb isn't called a 'vermifuge' – or worm-killer – for nothing. If you do try it, be careful not to overdo the herb: 16 ounces of boiling water poured over one or two ounces of dried tansy is the proper ratio. The following recipe is for tansy pudding, a close relation of baked custard:

| | |
|---|---|
| ¼ lb grounds almonds | rose flavouring |
| soft breadcrumbs | 1 tsp brandy |
| 3 oz fresh butter | lemon to taste |
| 2 tsp chopped tansy leaves | |

Mix all the ingredients together and pour onto them a pint of scalded milk. Add 4 beaten eggs, stir, and bake in a buttered dish for an hour.

Another old recipe suggests beating seven eggs together with two cups of cream, a pint of spinach juice, a little fresh tansy, half a cup of ground almonds, a glass of white wine and a pinch of nutmeg. Stirred together, the ingredients are baked in a pie crust.

# THYME
*Thymus serpyllum, T. vulgaris*

WRITERS HAVE ALWAYS had a soft spot for thyme, possibly because of the evocative nature of its name. (Unusually among herbs, thyme has no nicknames: a sprig of thyme is a sprig of thyme, sweet and plain.) Aristophanes knew it as a plant grown on graves; Virgil recommended pounding it with garlic to provide a source of energy to the men who scythed the summer grass for hay. Aristotle, observant as always, noticed that bees which have sipped nectar from thyme take a drink of water before starting work on the honeycomb. Practical Pliny recommended burning thyme to keep insects at bay. Duessa, the pretty witch in Edmund Spenser's *Faerie Queene*, was revealed in her true form of 'a filthy foul old woman' while bathing in her magical brew of thyme, 'oregon' and rue, and Keats's priest in *Endymion* carried a basket of cresses, thyme and lilies-of-the-valley to the woodland altar.

We all know that Titania was sleeping on a bank 'whereon the wild thyme blows' when Puck dropped the optically-deluding liquid on her lids, but gourmets might be more interested in a tip from one of the Three Musketeers. Porthos, in his old age, made sure his hares always had garden thyme to eat – not from kindness, but because of the delicate savour this gave their flesh. Francis Bacon gives us a hint of the smell of an Elizabethan garden with his famous recommendation that burnet, water-mints and thyme are best when trodden on and crushed: 'Therefore you are to set whole alleys of them, to have the pleasure when you walk or tread.' Now there's an idea to pursue.

Reading about herbs can make you quite wistful. There's Thomas Hardy's description of weary Mrs Yeobright, in *The Return of the Native*, sinking down on a patch of thyme to clear her head as well as rest her aching feet on a long walk, and it's strange for anyone living in the suburban wastelands of modern Nottinghamshire to realise how little time has passed since Paul Morel, in D.H. Lawrence's *Sons and Lovers*, took Miriam out after supper for a quick kiss on a bank of sweet thyme beside the river at Eastwood.

*Thumon* was the Greek for thyme, and thyme was the symbol of *thumos*, the spirit of force and courage; was this, perhaps, what ladies had in mind when they embroidered bees, famously partial to the herb, on their loved ones' scarves before sending them off to knock each other about in jousts? Before this, Roman soldiers bathed in thyme-scented water to increase their valour, while stay-at-home Romans used thyme as a flavouring for cheese.

Medicinally, thyme was a good all-round cure in Nicholas Culpeper's day, useful as a digestive and for hangovers, for whooping-cough, as a purge for catarrh and for any lung-connected illnesses. Today, as a tisane, it's still considered beneficial for coughs and digestion; thymol, a powerful antiseptic used in toothpaste and dressings, doesn't come from the common forms of thyme.

Easy to grow – the stonier the soil, the happier

and sweeter-smelling the plant, so long as it's well drained and gets some sun – thyme comes in more than a hundred species and named varieties. Lemon-scented thymes keep their leaves best in the winter, but the silver-leafed thymes are the toughest and have the best flavour. Dr Kitchener, an eccentric nineteenth-century cook, musician and astronomer for whom I have some respect, thought the delicious-smelling orange thyme (*T.* × *citriodorus* 'Fragrantissimus') was best for culinary purposes. Creole cooks use thyme in the mixture for blackening fish, together with oregano, garlic, paprika and white pepper. Dip the fish in molten butter, coat it with the spices and fry it fast.

You could, on the other hand, emulate the Ancient Egyptians, and try it out for a spot of home mummifying.

# VALERIAN
## *Valeriana officinalis*

THIS IS THE herbalists' valerian, not to be confused with gardeners' valerian, *Centranthus
ruber*. Derbyshire was the stronghold of the British
valerian industry throughout the nineteenth
century. The herb was grown only for its roots, and
the crop from a small field might be worth £75, an
impressive sum in the 1860s, when farming was, as
now, a perilous business.

Valerian appears in old books as 'fu' or 'phu', a
name which may allude to the bad smell of the
root-extracted oil. As its name was possibly derived
from the Latin *valere*, to fare well, it came to be
known as 'all heal' in English, and was grown in
monastic herb gardens.

The valerian so highly regarded in the Middle
East under the name of 'spikenard' belongs to
the Valerianaceae, but is a different plant, clearly
more fragrant, which provided a popular hair and
body oil, usually applied as a prelude to amorous
entanglements. It's difficult to know what Chaucer
had in mind when he described naughty Nicholas,
the clerk in *The Miller's Tale*, as 'himself sweet-
smelling as the root of licorice, valerian, or setwall.'
Perhaps he was remembering the vanilla-scented
flowers by which 'setwall' (because it likes to grow

by and into a wall), the English valerian, wins my affection.

Valerian is well-known to be irresistible to cats, but its similar hold over rats is less familiar – rumour goes that the Pied Piper of Hamelin always carried a sprig of valerian in his pockets. Charles Darwin, pondering the odours by which sexual attraction is signalled and answered, found valerian's astonishing hold over small felines worth study. The root is believed to be the source of their insatiable passion, and cats I've watched rolling on valerian certainly seem eager to get as close to the ground as possible.

Fabius Calumna, in 1592, cured himself of epilepsy with a tincture of valerian. Two centuries earlier, it had been recommended as an antidote to truculence: give valerian to any two combatants, the writer urged, and they would immediately become tranquil and lay down their weapons.

Valerian – think valium – is best known for its sedative powers, although it is not a narcotic. The root, when dried, produces an oil which, when heavily diluted, has almost miraculous effects. *Tinctura Valerianae ammoniata*, a mixture of the root oil with oil of nutmeg, lemon and ammonia, is the form in which Dr Charles Bovary probably administered it to his fretful wife Emma for her nerves; house-hospitals dealing with shell-shocked soldiers in the First World War used it; so did doctors faced with frightened civilians during the London Blitz, when valerian was a good seller in Mincing Lane market. Easily available in pill and tincture form, a valerian tisane (it should be drunk cold, heavily diluted) can also be made from the dried root. The taste can be slightly disguised by making the infusion with milk. If you want to grow your own crop, remember that it will have no value for your health until it is two years old.

Another name for valerian, capon's tail, has me baffled. So does the fact that it is used to flavour beers and certain ice-creams. It is not, so far as I know, esteemed by cooks.

# WOAD
## *Isatis tinctoria*

I HAVE LIKED woad ever since the day at primary
school when I was allowed to scrawl blue crayon
over a figure intended to represent a gallant Celt
defending his native shore. But the savage blue-
skinned Celt is a dubious figure, described by Julius
Caesar in *The Gallic Wars* after one brief visit to
Britain. Against the idea of woad being used to
intimidate invaders must be set Pliny's description
of Celtic women and children staining themselves
with blue dye when making sacrifices. This suggests
a mystical or religious connection, though the
practically-inclined might suspect that naked
humans also valued its power to repel stinging
insects. What is certain is that another venerable
country name, glastum, refers to the glorious dye
obtained from the leaves: *glaston* was the Old
Celtic word for it, and *glas* the Welsh word for
blue-grey. Thus Glastonbury, possibly 'place of the
blue', suggesting that woad may have been grown
there at one time. The Anglo-Saxon *wad* became
our woad and names like Wadborough in Worces-
tershire and Wadhill in Gloucestershire indicate
where the tall dye plant was grown. Gloucestershire
Dorset and Somerset, the chief ancient sites of
woad-growing, must have looked all the lovelier for

its presence, with its towering stems, foaming yellow flowers and the almost magical leaves which, as Richard Mabey gracefully says, 'seem to shine like stained glass with an inner, immanent blue'.

Perhaps it was this gleaming inner tint to the leaves which led the Celts to discover the woad plant's secret; otherwise, the question of how they worked out the complicated process by which a yellow-flowered plant with greenish leaves can be persuaded to produce a deep blue dye remains baffling.

The blue dye obtained from indigo gradually superseded that from woad during the seventeenth century, but by the sixteenth century woad production in England was already doomed, not only because the chemical process of producing its magnificent blue was so complicated and lengthy but because of the noxious smell. Modern woad-production is achieved with the help of sparkling ammonia, of which the cheap Elizabethan equivalent was urine. Queen Elizabeth herself had such a horror of the smell that she passed an edict against the making of woad dye at any town through which she was intending to pass. (The laws regarding the smells which might and might not reach the royal nostrils were breathtakingly detailed. If there is any connection between sensuality and sensitivity to smells, Elizabeth I was the Cleopatra of her age.)

A major drawback of woad as a commercial dye-plant is the amount of space it requires. An acre will produce a ton of it, and the leaves give a really good rich blue only during their first year, before the plants flower. (Experts can obtain beautiful shades of pink and grey by harvesting the leaves at certain times.) You could choose to grow woad for its looks alone, but bear two things in mind: nothing will grow happily in soil which has recently been used for woad, and it spreads so readily by means of its hanging black seeds that it has actually been banned in large parts of the United States, where it is categorised as a noxious weed. If you do choose to cultivate it, remember that woad only flowers in its second year, and that when it does, you should cut back all but one or two of the flowering stalks.

It is sad that woad production is so difficult and unfashionable, since all sources attest to the beauty of the colour it produces, and sad that, apart from colouring silks for Anatolian carpets, there seems to be no evidence of its commercial use nowadays. As the organic market flourishes and develops, this is an area which could be usefully explored.

# WORMWOOD
## *Artemisia absinthium*

WORMWOOD TAKES ITS botanical name, *Artemisia*, from the Greek name for the hunting goddess Diana, who roamed the woods and discovered the power of herbs – a hundred and eighty of them, to be precise – and then passed on the secret of their use to Chiron the Centaur, father of healing. If that story doesn't appeal, there was another Artemisia, sister and wife of King Mausolus and, in her spare time, a keen botanist.

Certainly wormwood has a venerable reputation. Ancient Egyptians used it – and it is still recommended by herbalists today – as the efficient worming medicine its popular name suggests. Roman wormwood, *Artemisia pontica*, a mild species, is used to add flavour to vermouth and campari, but common wormwood's more notorious use, as the second part of its name attests, is as a principal ingredient of absinthe. Banned in the USA in 1912 and in France in 1915, this licorice-flavoured aperitif was once the cool drink to enjoy at *l'heure verte*. Diluted by adding (iced) water over a sugar cube, and cautiously sipped, absinthe is reported to have a pleasant taste rather like Pernod. At 70° to 80° proof, it isn't a drink to be trifled with. A Dr Legrand, describing it in 1892 when the absinthe craze was at its height, offered a stern warning against the effects of over-indulgence. Intense thirst, vertigo and delusions would be followed, he threatened, by 'tremblings in the arms, hands and legs, and numbness of the extremities, loss of muscular power, delerium, loss of intellect, general paralysis, and death.'

But don't let this put you off the herb itself. Wormwood is both a great drawer of painted ladies (the butterfly variety) to the garden, and also an efficient moth repellent and insecticide. To make a wormwood tea mixture for use in the garden, boil 8 ounces of wormwood leaves and 1 teaspoon of Castile soap with 4 pints of water. Use it directly on insects and not, if you can help it, on young plants.

Although poisonous if taken in large quantities, wormwood enjoys an excellent press for its medicinal uses. The leaves and flowering shoots are good for almost anything you care to mention – you can make a warm compress for bruises, or chew them to stimulate the appetite (there are even reports of anorexia nervosa being treated successfully). Merely a sniff has a strange effect on some people, while others find it lives up to its reputation for calming the nerves. (Thujone, the constituent which connects it to marijuana as a mind-influencer, is also recognised as a brain stimulant.)

Culpeper was one of wormwood's most ardent fans. Commenting on 'Roman wormwood', he wondered why it was so-called, since it grew freely in England. Pretending to ponder the matter, he concluded that it must be because the herb cured 'a stinking breath, which the Romans cannot be free from, maintaining so many bad houses by authority of his Holiness.'

I'd be nervous of the Icelandic suggestion of rubbing honey and wormwood into the eyes to brighten them, but I can't resist passing on another Icelandic idea, that fountain-pen users should mix wormwood with their ink. Why? To keep mice from eating their pages.

The bitter taste of wormwood is proverbial; not even Mr Morel's loyal family, in *Sons and Lovers*, could bring themselves to taste his wormwood tea. The Book of Proverbs, issuing stern warnings about expensively available ladies, informs us that although their lips may drip honey and their words be smooth as oil, they all end by being 'as bitter as wormwood, sharp as a two-edged sword'. In the Book of Revelation, wormwood is the name of the third and cruellest of the stars that falls to earth at a trumpet's blast, and its evil gift is to contaminate the waters of the earth, making them impossible to drink. St John the Baptist adopted a girdle of wormwood to signify discipline. Rousseau, fondly remembering Madame Warens, sighed over the memory of how she had playfully smeared wormwood on his cheeks when he interrupted her medical work. Prince Andrew, struggling to blot out the horrors of war as he walked by the battlefield in *War and Peace*, counted his steps and sniffed a bunch of wormwood leaves. The ploy was effective.

Wormwood and its milder relation southernwood (*Artemisia abrotanum*) both do well in city gardens. A chemical-laden atmosphere suits them, and they deserve to play a significant role in town planners' schemes for 'greening-up' urban areas.

# YARROW
*Achillea millefolium*

Turn to the sixteenth-century book of *The Popol Vuh*, the extraordinary history of the Mayans' relationship with the gods, and you'll find yarrow and marigolds being burned with offerings of deerskins on the mountain altars. Deriving its common English name from the Anglo-Saxon *gearwe*, yarrow has been regarded since early times as one of the nine sacred herbs. This may have been on account of its magical powers or its medicinal properties, or both, since the history of magic and medicine is closely entwined: the power most often ascribed to witches was that of inflicting illness on a victim, and yarrow was famous for keeping illness at bay.

Chiron the Centaur is said to have taught the skill of staunching wounds with yarrow's silky-haired leaves to Achilles, who passed the information on to his followers, earning the herb its Latin name *Achillea*. Druids used it, somehow (their trick has not been passed down), to forecast the weather, but yarrow remains more famous for its use as nature's best bandage on the battlefield. This explains its names soldier's woundwort and *Herba Militaris*.

'Old man's pepper' recalls that yarrow was used

as a cheap form of snuff, and that it can bring on a nosebleed if a leaf is pushed up a nostril, as suggested for easing certain forms of migraine. Used in this way, yarrow can also indicate your romantic situation. 'Yarroway, yarroway, bear a white flower,' you must say while sniffing the broad daisy-flowered head, 'if my love love me, my nose will bleed now.' You may be kept waiting: 'If [yarrow] be put into the nose,' wrote the herbalist John Parkinson, 'assuredly it will stay the bleeding of it.'

Yarrow was taken to America by the first settlers, who depended on it as a cure for cuts and colds, only to find relatives of the plants they brought with them already in use among the Indian tribes of the East Coast. The Potawatomi kept evil spirits away by laying yarrow flowers on hot coals, while dancers and magicians chewed yarrow roots before holding hot coals in their mouths for as long as a minute.

Dr Thornton, writing in 1810, reported that bruises caused by a severe fall from a tree had been completely cured by the application of yarrow poultices, and there are many other tributes to its power as an anti-inflammatory (Linnaeus found it being drunk as a cure for rheumatism in Norway). Many old herbals suggest a warm yarrow rinse to prevent baldness, and chewing the fresh leaves is said to alleviate toothache. Yarrow's most impressive modern reputation, however, is as a cold cure. Some suggest an infusion of the dried plant, but the most enthusiastic account prefers an infusion of the fresh leaves, with peppermint and elderflower added if you wish. Taken just before going to bed, this will bring on a sweat and, it is said, break even the most severe cold.

Culpeper, who places it under Venus's care, gives yarrow a good report as a remedy for sexual diseases. 'It helps the gonorrhoea in men, and the whites in women,' he says, and also remarks on its value as a cure for incontinence.

Given all these helpful properties, it seems hard that yarrow should also be called devil's nettle and bad man's plaything; forget such unkind descriptions and turn its dried flowers and leaves into ingredients for a home facial. Add a tablespoon each of fennel seeds and mint leaves and two tablespoons each of lavender and yarrow to a bowl of boiling water, and steam your face for five minutes with a towel draped over your head and the bowl. You'll glow like a hot-house peach afterwards, I promise.

On a more mundane note, try adding a few chopped yarrow leaves to any garden compost that is slow to rot. Proving just how powerful herbs can be, two small yarrow leaves can activate as much as a full cubic yard of compost.

Pretty in the garden when it has formed a large clump, topped through most of the summer by tiny bright pink flowers, yarrow will also help its neighbours thrive. What more, really, could you ask of a herb which we still tend to treat as a weed?